WHY I RUN
The remarkable journey of the ordinary runner

By Mark Sutcliffe

Great River Media, Inc. | Ottawa

Mark Sutcliffe is a writer, broadcaster and entrepreneur who lives in Ottawa with his wife, Ginny, and their children, Erica, Jack and Bump, who is due in August 2011.

Mark is the founder of iRun, Canada's most popular running magazine and website. He hosts iRun's weekly radio show and podcast and has written regularly about running for more than five years in the Ottawa Citizen and in his blog at iRun.ca.

A runner since 1998, he ran his first half-marathon in 2003 and his first marathon in 2004. He has completed eleven marathons and has raised more than $50,000 for local and national charities through running and other fundraising efforts.

Mark is also an accomplished print, radio and television journalist. He writes two columns per week in the Citizen, hosts the Chat Room, a top-rated morning talk show on Ottawa's news-talk radio station 580 CFRA; The Week, a national Sunday morning political television show on CPAC; and Talk Ottawa, a local issues program airing three times a week on Rogers Television.

Mark is the CEO of Great River Media Inc., which publishes iRun, the Ottawa Business Journal, the Kitchissippi Times community newspaper and several other publications.

Mark was recently named volunteer fundraiser of the year at the Ottawa Philanthropy Awards and volunteer of the year by the Great Canadian Theatre Company.

Published in Canada by Great River Media, Inc. Ottawa in 2011

ISBN: 978-0-9868242-0-3

Manuscript edited by Bruce Deachman and Karen Karnis

Art Direction: Lisa Georges

Design and production: Greg Cosgrove

Photo credits:

Page 36: Bonnie Findley

Page 40, 72, 88, 128, 176, 200, 204, 224, 236, 280, 292, 296: Mark Sutcliffe

Page 48, 76: Colin Rowe

Page 64: Paul Yates

Pages 84, 104, 116: Sandra Laurin

Page 108: Rick Smith

Page 260: Zoomphoto.ca

Page 272: impossible2Possible

Page 12, 100, 144, 288: Courtesy of Mark Sutcliffe

Printed in Canada

[TABLE OF CONTENTS]

[FOREWORD BY MALCOLM GLADWELL]

I started running when I was twelve because I wanted to run races. At that age, it seemed to me to be the point. The summer before I turned thirteen I remember running up and down a farmer's track, behind our house, in competition with my brother and my father. We would stagger each person's starting point, according to some elaborate calculation of individual handicap, and time each interval with a big, old-fashioned stopwatch. My goal, at first, was to beat my brother. Then it was to beat my father. And then, when I entered high school and ran track and cross-country, it was to beat as many people as possible in my age group. Running was a competitive activity, like Monopoly or playing cards, for which the only appropriate goal was victory. Once, after winning a cross-country race in high school, I remember my coach asking me if I liked running, and I was utterly bewildered by the question. I had won, hadn't I? And I won a lot in those years — local races, provincial races — and that was always my answer. Until, at the grand old age of fifteen, I abruptly stopped winning — and all of a sudden I had to decide how I really felt.

In the pages that follow, Mark Sutcliffe will tell you stories about his own running experiences. Superficially, they are nothing at all like mine. He came to running late. I started early.

He runs marathons. I was a miler as a kid, and to this day regard races at lengths greater than ten kilometres to be acts of lunacy. We actually went running once and, predictably, he would have been happier going longer and slower and I would have been happier going shorter and faster. But beneath those surface differences, our stories — like all running stories — are very similar. They are all reflections on running's great paradox: that this most elemental and primal of human activities is also deeply (and occasionally frustratingly) complex.

How, for example, could I not know whether I liked running? Hockey players don't wonder whether they like hockey. Of course, they like hockey. Hockey's great virtue is that it is inherently likeable. Running is not. It is painful and demanding and difficult and frustrating. I did not run for another three years, after my peak at fifteen. Then I began again, in fits and starts, through my twenties and early thirties. But each comeback attempt would founder on the question of why. Remind me why again I'm killing myself in the pouring rain, on some lonely road? Slowly, though, over the course of many miles, I began to work out my answer. I began to realize that something that was painful and demanding and difficult and frustrating could also be beautiful and incredibly satisfying — not in spite of its pain and difficulty but because of it: that those things that come with effort and sacrifice are infinitely more meaningful as a result. What I did not grasp until I was much older was how miraculous running is. You don't see it at fourteen or fifteen, when physical activity is a given. But now, in my mid-forties, I see it plain as day: that a fully grown adult can go out and run continuously and happily for forty-five minutes is something that — every time I do it — never ceases to astound me.

Am I sounding like one of those tiresome running gurus?

Perhaps. And do all runners think of running this way? Maybe not. I suspect that anyone capable of running forty-two kilometres — like Mark — is a bit less conflicted about this particular form of human activity. But I think Mark would agree — and I hope you do as well as you read through this marvellous collection of essays — there is much to be said, and much to be learned, from the deceptively simple act of putting on a pair of training shoes and venturing out onto the roads. Enjoy.

[INTRODUCTION]

iRun because it has changed my life! REBECCA BROWN, ONTARIO

One night not too long ago, my wife, Ginny, and I were lying in bed, having one of our regular discussions to sort out who was going to do what and when. I was providing details on the small number of available spots in my schedule that were left over after my two main activities in life, work and training, when she said rather bluntly, "Running is non-negotiable for you."

As a chronic procrastinator who has sometimes struggled with commitment, and who fears letting running and other priorities slip if I lose control over my time, I took it as a compliment.

I'm fairly certain, however, she didn't intend it as one. It wasn't said with a tone that suggested, "Hey, running is non-negotiable for you – way to go!" or "One of the things I love about you is that running is non-negotiable for you."

To be honest, it sounded more like, "Why haven't you cleaned out the basement yet?"

But considering one of my greatest fears is not having the discipline to stay on track with something important, I couldn't help but feel a little bit proud that I'm inflexible about my running habit.

I chose to keep that reaction to myself, however. Ginny is a runner too, and one of my favourite runs ever was finishing a half-marathon by her side in 2008. But managing our busy lives and giving birth to our kids have made it tough for her to be as unbendable about running as I am.

Through running and many other activities, I've learned this much: I don't have a dimmer switch. It's either on or off, rarely in between. So when I commit to something, I go all in. And I check myself regularly against the risk of an excuse creeping in that will derail my plans.

On days I don't run, I'm already thinking ahead to when I will fit in my training the next day. I'm not sure if that's discipline; it feels more like anxiety that I will fall behind.

From experience, I know all the justifications you can employ to delay, avoid, ignore, postpone, cancel: it's a bad week, I'm busy with work, it's too cold, it's too hot, I'm not feeling well, I'll start next week.

I fear the slippery slope that starts with just one cancelled run. It starts with a week when I don't get in my minimum four runs. Next comes a week with only one or two. And then all of a sudden I'm not running at all. That sequence of events has never happened, but I still worry that it will.

So, Ginny is right. Running is non-negotiable. There are a lot of things I'd give up, including sleep, before I'd give up one of my scheduled runs.

But it didn't start out that way. Frankly, I find it extraordinary to call myself a runner, to be someone whose inflexibility over training for a half-marathon or marathon would be an inconvenience to the important people in my life, someone who gets asked regularly, "Did you run today?" by a large number of people who are aware of my obsession.

My parents were not into sports, so I wasn't a particularly active kid. I played little league baseball and shot some hoops at the park across the street. But I didn't run track or cross-country in high school. There were no trophies or medals in my bedroom as a teenager (except one or two for math). The best word to describe my relationship with sports at that time in my life would have been "spectator."

A friend in high school trained for the Ottawa Marathon one year and I thought it was an utterly unachievable task, something only a superhuman could do. I asked him a lot of questions about it, but I found it impossible to grasp the distance or the training commitment. I tried running a few times as a teenager but I usually ran too fast too soon and ended up coughing up a lung about five blocks from home.

In the late 1980s, I covered the Ottawa Marathon for the local radio station I worked for. I remember being impressed enough to consider training for the marathon the following year, but I never got started. But my experience covering the race did lead to a misunderstanding that lasted for several years.

When I told an acquaintance that I had thoroughly enjoyed watching the marathon, he said, "A bunch of us are going down to the New York Marathon this year. You should join us."

For some reason I assumed he meant they were going to watch the race, not run in it. So I said, "Sure. Sounds great." A week later, he sent me an application form.

I found some way to get out of going, but for the next few years whenever I ran into him, he would ask, "How's the running going?" and I would mutter something about not having had time to run recently.

Many years later, I did become a runner. But I'm not a particularly special one. I'm not, for example, one of those lucky people who discovered, upon taking up running as adults, that they were incredibly fast. The only time I've broken the tape at a finish line was at an event where I was the only participant. I'm certainly not an elite athlete.

I haven't defied the odds to become a runner. I'm not a cancer survivor. I didn't lose 100 pounds in one year. I didn't overcome a serious disability, illness or injury to run a marathon.

I'm just an ordinary guy who, like so many others, started running as a form of exercise and discovered, much to my surprise, an activity I grew to love so much that it became part of my way of life, a non-negotiable part, it turns out.

Along the way, however, I discovered something I never expected: that the journey of a runner is remarkable even if the runner isn't.

I started running in my thirties, just to stay in shape. By the time I ran my first marathon, in 2004, I was hooked. Running has become for me a hobby, a challenge, a tonic, a social activity, a creative outlet. It is often a source of joy and sometimes a cause of extreme frustration.

I'm thinner than I was before and I feel like I'm in much better shape, but otherwise running has not transformed me physically. Nevertheless, it has dramatically altered me both emotionally and spiritually.

As a child and teenager, I lacked confidence. I questioned my own fortitude. I even thought of myself as a bit of a wimp sometimes. In running, however, especially in those final few kilometres of a half-marathon or marathon, I discovered something new about myself, a toughness and persistence I didn't know was there.

It's impossible to overstate the impact of that discovery on me and many other runners I've talked to. It's amazing what running farther than you ever thought possible will do to your perception of yourself and the path in front of you. I don't know how many times I've said to myself in the last seven years, when approaching a challenging task, "If I can run a marathon, surely I can do this."

Having witnessed that transformation in myself and many others, I was inspired to start writing about running. It led to a weekly column in the *Ottawa Citizen*, then the launch of *iRun*, a national magazine and website for Canadian runners, and a weekly radio show and podcast about running. And, ultimately, to this book.

In the pages ahead, I explore my path from the sideline to the starting line, from motionlessness to the marathon, in a series of running stories which I've written over the past five years. Each stands alone, so you don't have to read them in any particular order. But together, they chronicle my personal journey as a runner.

A big part of that passage has been the inspiring runners I've met along the way: elite athletes such as Dean Karnazes, Silvia Ruegger, Simon Whitfield and Adam van Koeverden; runners who have made spectacular comebacks from illness or injury, such as Rick Ball, Jody Mitic and Shelby Hayter; and everyday runners doing extraordinary things, including Rick Rayman, Gavin Lumsden and Shelley Morris.

You'll read about the day I started calling myself a runner, what it was like stumbling through the woods on my first significant trail run, and the joy I had in seeing my closest friend qualify for the Boston Marathon, something I have yet to do.

And I'll tell you what it was like running, at least until he left me behind, with Malcolm Gladwell, who wrote the foreword to this book.

I'll also wade into some minor running controversies: Boston qualifying times, headphones in races and deaths at major marathon events. There is a lot about what inspires me, and what I hope will inspire you as well.

In the pages ahead, I try to provide a fresh perspective on the life of an everyday runner, one that is uniquely Canadian (watch for lots of references to kilometres and Terry Fox and winter). I believe the journey of a runner is very similar no matter how fast or how often it's travelled, so I think there's something here for everyone, from the novice to the experienced, from someone who runs 5k three times a week to the person training for an ultramarathon.

Throughout this book, you'll also see a series of iRun statements, from among the thousands of one-sentence assertions about why we run that have been sent in from runners across Canada and around the world since we launched the magazine. Those small glimpses into the soul of other runners have always inspired me to carry on both running and writing about it.

Although I cover a lot of my own running experiences and profile the runners who have inspired me, I don't think this book is just about me and them. If you run, I believe it's also about you. Everyone who puts on a pair of running shoes makes a choice to move faster and farther than they would otherwise in everyday life. For me, it's been a transformative decision.

I suspect you'll find my journey a familiar one. The details may be different, but the story of every runner has similar themes and milestones. In running we discover many things. I've tried to explore as many of those as possible as I share my love of the sport that has changed my life.

On the day I finished the final piece of writing for this book, I put on my gear to go for a short celebratory run. My son Jack, who was twenty-two months old, looked at me in my running shoes and said, for the first time in his life, "Daddy run."

This is why I do.

[**RUNNING FORWARD, LOOKING BACK**]

iRun for my past, now and future MONICA ANTHONY, ONTARIO

According to clichés and rock songs, you're not supposed to look back. Looking back is associated with regret, remorse and other unhealthy instincts. Indeed, in running and life it's better to be facing forward than looking over your shoulder.

But sometimes, as long as you're not in the middle of a crowded race or on a trail run through the forest or wallowing in self-pity, it can be helpful to look at the road behind you. You may find it reassuring to see how far you've come.

I used to keep track of almost every single time I exercised (I can't help it, I'm like that). So one day, when I happened to stumble upon my training log from 2001, it was a chance to look into a bit of a runner's time capsule.

In March 2001, I couldn't call myself a runner. I was just a guy trying to stay in shape. Mostly I went to the gym and rode a stationary bike while reading the morning newspaper (that's how strenuous it was) and lifted a few very light weights. My goal was to get about thirty minutes of exercise four or five times a week. In other words, the bare minimum.

I ran sometimes, usually on a treadmill and once in a while, when the weather was good, outside. But even when I ran, I didn't call it running. In early April 2001, according to my training log, I went "jogging" for half an hour.

Jogging is a word I have not used in a long time. According to Wikipedia, jogging is "a form of trotting or running at a slow or leisurely pace." Yeah, that pretty much describes me at the turn of the century. Trotting. Slow. Leisurely.

In 2001, running wasn't part of my vocabulary, much less my lifestyle or my career. I had never even considered running in a race, so there wasn't a collection of number bibs and finish-line photos stuck on a wall in my den. Wet and smelly running clothes weren't hanging from every banister in the house. I didn't know what a personal best was, let alone have one at any distance. Gift certificates from running stores were not the default birthday and Christmas presents from close family.

When I ran – or jogged – I wore a lot of grey and white cotton. I looked like Rocky in that famous scene when he climbs the steps of the Philadelphia Museum of Art, only slower and less inspiring. I usually wore a ball cap from the Baseball Hall of Fame. I don't know what brand of shoes I wore, but they were the same ones I used to play squash.

A marathon? That was for crazy people. I got in my car and mapped out two 5k routes through my neighbourhood and figured that would be as far as I would ever need to go. Once in a while, I would get really ambitious and tack on an extra kilometre or so, noting it carefully in my log.

Somewhere far in the future, I would finally stop writing down every single run. By then I had a fancy watch that was recording them all anyway. But I think running became such a regular part of my life that it didn't seem worth noting anymore. I don't keep a sleeping log. I don't write down every time I go to work. Why would I record all my runs?

(There is one other major difference between then and now, according to my training log: after every single run in 2001, I did a lot of stretching.)

But at the start of the new millennium, I was, by my own description, a jogger.

On April 22, 2001, I entered my first event, a 5k race. I enjoyed the experience, but that's not when I got hooked. I didn't do another race for more than two years.

Back then, I didn't expect I would ever be a serious runner, with all the wick-away gear and gadgets, much less somebody who wrote, spoke and published a magazine about running. But somewhere along the way, something changed, other than the fact that I stopped stretching after my runs.

In that exercise log from 2001, I start using the word "running" in September. I don't know whether it was because I was getting a little bit more serious about it, or whether "jogging" just didn't sound cool enough anymore.

It would be another six months before I decided one day, on a whim towards the end of my regular run, to do a second lap and run ten kilometres for the first time in my life (I figured it would be easier to decide to do a 10k run when I'd already run 5k than when I was starting from home). It would be almost another two years before I would run my first half-marathon, still draped in cotton and a baseball cap. My first winter of running outside was a few years away. And my first marathon, and that moment when Running Room founder John Stanton referred to me and all the others crossing the finish line as "runners" and "athletes" and I thought, "Yeah, I'm a runner" – that was almost three years in the future.

It's powerful to see how far you can travel in a relatively short period of time, literally one step at a time. When someone says to me, "I could never be a runner," I always point out I didn't start out as one either.

Because somewhere between March and September of 2001, I stopped jogging and started running. And until now, I have never looked back.

[**WHY I RUN**]

iRun for no particular reason SCOTT MOORE, ONTARIO

Because it can give you an ache in your legs that you feel with every step, and you love it because you know you've earned it, because you've just done something hard.

Because it is hard.

Because you can take it anywhere, on business trips, on vacations, to the cottage.

Because you don't have to book a court or make a date with a partner. You don't need any equipment except your shoes.

Because it clears your head.

Because it makes you feel like you're cheating the aging process.

Because you can use it to justify eating almost anything you want.

Because you can do it by yourself, with a friend, in small groups or large.

Because you can learn a new little technique and try it out and always hang on to the hope you can get a little bit better.

Because when there's madness all around you and you've had an incredibly frustrating day, it can help you put everything back in perspective.

Because you don't need to pay a membership fee or wait in line for a machine.

Because you can do it while you watch the sun going up or down.

Because you can do it before the sun comes up and feel like you're ahead of the game.

Because you can do it after the sun goes down and taste the crisp night air and feel cool and warm at the same time.

Because you can set a goal and if you achieve it, it's unequivocal, unambiguous, absolute and total and complete, unlike almost anything else in life.

Because it makes you go outside, on good days and bad, even in the winter, and you can do it in the rain or the wind or the snow or some combination of all of them and it makes you feel tough and hearty, which you never thought you were.

Because since you never pictured yourself training for three hours at a time, it shows there's another level to you that you can get to if you go about it the right way.

Because it proves you aren't hardwired at birth, that you can decide you're going to be athletic or anything else, that who you are is completely up to you.

Because seeing other people doing it, the moms and middle-aged men, the kids, the seniors, all testing their limits, gives you inspiration.

Because even if you're not really that fast, you have a competitive streak and this is something you can measure, and if you can just go a bit faster than last time, or someone else who looks like he's in pretty good shape, that feels pretty good.

Because it makes you think about your breathing.

Because it makes you feel like you have something in common with world-class athletes, like you can understand what they're going through; because even though you'll never win anything, you know what it is to train for something.

Because no matter how much of a team player or mother or father or partner you want to be, there have to be some things that belong to you and nobody else.

Because no matter how little sense this makes to someone who's never tried it, sometimes you have more energy after than before.

Because you can finish a race faster than you've ever done before and it doesn't matter who's ahead or behind, you beat the old you.

Because of that time your family came out holding a sign with your name on it and shouted cheers to you when you went past.

And especially because of those times when you stretch it out at the end, just take it up a little bit faster, feel the wind in your lungs, feel like you're reaping all the training you've ever done, feel your heart pumping faster, your whole system operating at maximum capacity, the adrenaline flowing, making you feel alive, and you know that feeling's going to stay with you for an hour after you stop.

That's why I run.

[DIANNE, DAD, MONEY]

iRun because it helps me raise money for charities FRANK FOTIA, ONTARIO

It's hard to remember exactly where and when it began, this crazy little obsession of mine.

How does a bit of running to stay in shape turn into a half-marathon, then a marathon, then an utterly non-negotiable part of every week, a bigger priority than sleeping or reading?

What was the turning point? When did I become a runner, rather than simply someone who ran? When did it go from an activity to being part of the definition of who I am? I ride my bike, I swim, I walk, I play other sports. Still, I don't call myself a cyclist or a walker or a ballplayer. But I am a runner.

In 2003, when running was still just one piece of my fitness regimen, I figured I would try doing a half-marathon. It would give me something to train for and it would be a test of endurance. Lots of other people were doing it, so why couldn't I?

For a novice runner who is attempting a new distance, whether it's 5k or a marathon or anything in between, there is only one question: Will I finish? I remember having breakfast with a friend when I was approaching the end of my training. One day we would run together four times a week and finish races side by side. But at this time, I was a rookie and he was an Ironman, which is why we were meeting for breakfast instead of going for a run.

Still uncertain about whether I could run 21.1 kilometres, I told him about my recent 18k training run.

"You've got it!" he said enthusiastically. I didn't believe him.

But on race day, I just kept putting one foot in front of the other and I ran farther than I ever thought possible.

Now I was a guy who had done a half-marathon. But I still wasn't a runner.

In fact, that fall I walked the Terry Fox Run. It wasn't that I couldn't have run the distance, but I was with someone who wanted to walk, so I did too. Simple as that. Today, however, I would be wishing that person luck and meeting her at the finish line.

The next spring, I toyed with training for the marathon, or as I called it then, from the perspective of a half-marathoner, the "full" marathon.

Even though thousands of other people had done it, I wasn't sure I could. I finally convinced myself to join a marathon clinic by settling on a giant exit clause: I could train for the marathon and switch to the half if I found it too hard.

Over the next four months, I soaked up every aspect of the marathon training experience. I did every prescribed run in the training program except for maybe two short runs I skipped because of a cold. I attended almost every talk at the clinic.

It was a time in my life when I need a fixation, a routine, a diversion. My sister had died only eighteen months earlier and my father was terminally ill.

And so I did one more thing that made me slightly more committed to the marathon: I turned my run into a fundraiser for the Ottawa Hospital, where both of them had received treatment. And before I knew it, I had raised almost $10,000. Backing out wasn't going to be as easy as I originally planned.

I was encouraged by my training, but I still had my doubts. What if I hit this wall that I had heard about? What were the last ten kilometres, the ones we didn't do in training, going to be like? What if I just had to stop? What if no matter how much I trained, I just didn't have a marathon in me?

The clinic instructors provided a helpful talk about motivation. They told me to prepare for the point when the race would get incredibly hard, when my body would tell me to quit and I would have to keep going. Think now about what you will think about then, they said.

I came up with a plan: I would remember my sister, my dad and all the money I had raised in their names. That should be enough to keep me going.

"Dianne, Dad, money." That's what I was going to repeat to myself every three steps when I needed that push. "Dianne, Dad, money."

At the start line, I reassured myself with the promise that tens of thousands of other runners have made before their first marathon: You only have to do this once. Check it off the list and you never have to run this far again for the rest of your life.

I remember the exact point when the race really began. It was on a long slow uphill stretch after a steep climb over a bridge at 32k.

I stopped running and walked for a hundred metres. "Dianne, Dad, money," I thought to myself. Then I started running again.

I'd like to say that surge of inspiration was enough to carry me to the finish, that I felt like angels wings were lifting me off the ground, but I walked several more times. And at one point, I even rationalized stopping completely. What – is everyone going to ask for their money back, I thought. It's going to a hospital, for crying out loud. It's not going to me.

But I put those thoughts out of my mind and pushed on to 40k. My mom and aunt were standing on a bridge holding a sign with my name on it. That spurred me on for a few hundred metres.

Dianne, Dad, money.

I don't remember much about the final stretch or crossing the finish line, except that I almost started crying. It was more relief than jubilation.

Just after the finish I ran into a friend who had completed many marathons. "Congratulations," he said. "By the way, now is not the time to decide if you want to run another marathon."

I smiled and didn't respond. But I think I'd already decided.

I was back again the next year and the year after that.

I don't know exactly when I became totally hooked on this foolish passion, when running became part of me instead of me simply being part of a race.

But I like to think the turning point was in those final few kilometres of my first marathon, when I drew on the inspiration of my sister and father and the dozens of people who believed enough in me to contribute a few dollars toward my race.

Somewhere on the long, slow uphill climb, I stopped doubting I could finish and started believing I was a runner.

[**A GREAT RUNNING NATION**]

iRun because it's cheaper than playing hockey ELI ADAMSON, ONTARIO

To those who think this is a hockey country, I say Canada is a nation of runners. We're home to thousands and thousands who train in some of the toughest elements in the world. We have a rich history of champions and record-breakers. And one Canadian is simply the greatest runner of all time.

True, we may not have won as many international track meets as hockey tournaments. And Canadians may not be the favourites at any of the major marathons. But this is still the country that sent Tom Longboat to victory in Boston and Donovan Bailey to a gold medal in Atlanta. And produced dozens of other great champions in between.

This is a land with as many as a million runners. That's about double the number of hockey players. And many Canadians run all year round in one of the most extreme climates on the planet. Show me another country where you train for a marathon when it's minus-30 and run the event when it's plus-25, all in the same city.

Still not convinced? Consider this: when the people of this country were asked by a TV network to vote on the Greatest Canadian, the guy who came second (and should have won) was a runner. If you were to ask Canadians of any age to name their biggest Canadian hero, a huge number would name that runner. What other country (except maybe Kenya) can say that?

Many have run faster than Terry Fox. A small few have run farther. But no other runner in human history combines his incredible athletic achievement and the impact he continues to have on millions of lives around the world. Who else could have even conceived of running across the world's second largest country on only one leg?

Through the simple yet profound act of running, for 143 days and more than 5,000 kilometres, Terry Fox transformed the way people think, inspired millions of people and launched a legacy that will last a century and beyond.

Terry's legacy has spread farther than he ever dreamed. Since the Marathon of Hope in 1980, more than $400 million has been raised for cancer research in his name. There have been Terry Fox Runs in fifty countries around the world. Name another runner who is known everywhere from Argentina and Australia, by kids who weren't even born when he died.

Terry died in 1981 at the age of twenty-two. Although he didn't live to see it, he knew about the first Terry Fox Run. Could he have imagined more than thirty? It's hard to believe, but the Terry Fox Run is now older than Terry Fox was.

Try to conjure a picture of Terry Fox at fifty, which he would have turned in 2008. It's almost impossible. Terry Fox will always be the picture of youthful nerve and determination. Indeed, an image of that sunburnt kid is ingrained into the highest level of the Canadian consciousness. The Terry Fox we know just wouldn't do as a middle-aged guy. Terry isn't ageless, he's permanently young.

But time has marched on since Terry's Marathon of Hope ended on Sept. 1, 1980. There are kids in school today whose parents were children when Terry died. Thankfully, Terry Fox is as much a hero to them as he was to the people who witnessed his incredible journey. Considering Terry was gone long before the Internet, text-messaging and *American Idol*, that's saying something.

As just one of millions of examples, seven-year-old Samantha Clarke raised $100 for the Terry Fox Run in 2008 after her grandfather died of cancer. In the year following that, she raised $9,000 more. She sold off her toys and even asked her family to give her money for cancer research at Christmas, instead of gifts.

Terry Fox started with a dream of raising one dollar per Canadian for cancer research. By the time he died he had already made his goal, some $25 million raised from a population of twenty-four million.

The Terry Fox Run is a race like no other. You don't even have to show up at the beginning of the race to participate. Nor do you have to run the Terry Fox Run. Just be there sometime that day and walk, run, bike, wheel or rollerblade ten kilometres.

No one will check if you've walked the entire course and there are no timing devices. But pretend you're a cancer survivor with only one leg and picture yourself doing some forty kilometres a day for 143 days. Then 10k might not seem like so much.

No runner on earth has made a greater impression on so many people than Terry Fox. That's why Canada is not only a great running nation, it's home to the greatest runner of all time.

[REACHING THE TIPPING POINT]

iRun because running gives me so much in return TERRY SANCARTIER, QUEBEC

"What happened to you?"

It's not very often I get this question from my wife at the end of an 8k run. But it's not very often I return from a short run with my shirt absolutely soaked with sweat and looking like I just ran for my life from a family of bears.

What happened to me was Malcolm Gladwell. The brainiac best-selling author was in Ottawa in June 2009 for a United Way event at which I was given the privilege of interviewing him onstage at the National Arts Centre.

Gladwell is renowned for his thought-provoking, analytical research and powerful storytelling that have yielded the hugely successful books *The Tipping Point*, *Blink* and *Outliers*. But long before he was a champion of non-fiction, Gladwell was a top-ranked middle-distance runner. As a teenager, he was Ontario's best 1,500-metre runner and set a Canadian record in his age category.

In our brief chat before we went on stage, I asked him if he was still running. Gladwell said chronic knee problems limited him to about forty minutes per run, but he still got out several times a week.

As a matter of fact, he added, he was planning to go for a run that evening in Ottawa, once our event was over.

Really?

But he wasn't sure where to run. He knew of the path along Ottawa's Rideau Canal, but because of his knees he wanted to run somewhere that offered a softer running surface alongside the path.

I told him about the route along the Ottawa River, starting at the locks behind the Château Laurier. It's scenic, secluded and, unlike the canal path, lined with grass. And, sensing an opportunity, I offered to join him if he wanted a tour guide.

We had a brief discussion about pace, which is the runner's equivalent of a speed-dating conversation: a quick determination of compatibility. Gladwell modestly suggested he might be too slow for me, but I wasn't buying it.

"Did you run competitively in high school or university?" Gladwell asked me before we set off.

Uh, no. My main sport in high school was the Reach for the Top quiz-show team.

After translating miles into kilometres, we determined, not surprisingly, that his casual pace was the same as a tempo run for me. So, if we weren't ideal running partners, we were at least compatible. We agreed to meet at the front door of his hotel later in the evening.

Once our event was over, I raced home to change into running gear and got back just in time. We took the steps down to the locks and started off at a quick but manageable pace. At least that's what it was for me.

I asked Gladwell about his running career, and he said he gave up competitive running when he realized there were other athletes who were willing to push themselves to painful places more often and for longer than he was. He asked me about my writing and my running magazine, and I noticed it was a lot harder for me to get my words out than it had been for him.

And that was before he started speeding up.

If you think Malcolm Gladwell can give your mind a workout, wait until you run with him. As he picked up the tempo, the sweat started pouring down my face, while he continued to look like he was in the middle of a pleasant stroll. He would get a metre or two ahead of me and I would fight my way back to stay even, maybe because he would politely slow down or maybe because I was cutting the corners on the route.

In my defence, I had already run that morning and also biked downtown and back. And normally when I run at this pace, I'm not usually trying to maintain an interesting discussion with one of my writing heroes. Normally when I do a tempo run, I'm trying to get value from the workout, not the conversation.

Not that I would have kept up with him even if I'd tapered for a week. I told him I normally run with a chartered accountant and public-policy consultant who's ten years older than me, not a former 1,500-metre record-holder with ancestry similar to Usain Bolt.

I hung on for as long as I could, but about six kilometres into the run, when the finish line was straight ahead and I no longer had to supply directions, I politely suggested to Gladwell that he go ahead and I would meet him at the end of our route.

On the stretch behind the Parliament Buildings, I settled into a more comfortable pace and watched him slowly build up the distance between us until he disappeared around a corner.

Running with Malcolm Gladwell was a treat and a privilege. But let's just say I had reached the tipping point.

[BLAME PHEIDIPPIDES]

iRun to carry the message DEREK CARTER, ALBERTA

Is it a guy named Pheidippides we should blame for this?

Or is it some ancient Greek writer who embellished a nugget of history into a piece of melodramatic fiction?

Or should we fault poet Robert Browning and two of his followers: a baron and the father of modern semantics? While we're at it, should we curse the British Royal Family for those torturous final few metres?

Marathon runners owe their agony and glory to a compelling but utterly fictional story about an Athenian herald.

The myth goes that in 490 B.C., Pheidippides ran from the battlefield of Marathon to Athens, a distance of about forty-two kilometres, to announce a Greek triumph over Persia. After shouting, "We were victorious!" he died on the spot. Apparently he didn't hydrate enough during his run.

The truth is, Pheidippides was a better runner than that. According to Herodotus, he ran from Athens to Sparta, a distance of about 250 kilometres, in two days.

Along the way, he encountered a god named Pan; their conversation led to Pan helping the Athenians win the Battle of Marathon. This may explain the later confusion of the story of Pheidippides with the battlefield of Marathon. It also may be the first reported case of hallucinations experienced by a tired long-distance runner.

Over the next 500 years, the story evolved into the legend we know today. Perhaps it was adjusted by a Greek author who was the forefather of the writers of made-for-TV movies. Anyone who runs marathons should give thanks that someone got the story wrong and they're not being challenged to do a "Sparta" of 250 kilometres.

In 1879, Browning wrote of Pheidippides:

So, when Persia was dust, all cried, "To Acropolis!
Run, Pheidippides, one race more! the meed is thy due!
Athens is saved, thank Pan, go shout!" He flung down his shield
Ran like fire once more: and the space 'twixt the fennel-field
And Athens was stubble again, a field which a fire runs through,
Till in he broke: "Rejoice, we conquer!" Like wine through clay,
Joy in his blood bursting his heart, he died – the bliss!

Browning never may have covered the distance himself, but at least he understood then, as thousands will today, the joy felt when after running forty-two kilometres, you finally get to stop. And whenever you're watching others run, remember to cheer by shouting, "The meed is thy due!"

Stirred by the poem, the French semantics expert Michel Breal suggested to his friend Baron Pierre de Coubertin that a forty-kilometre race be added to the first modern Olympic Games in 1896 in Athens. Breal's participation is appropriate: semantics is defined as the study of meaning, and some marathon runners find themselves searching for meaning at about thirty-seven kilometres.

De Coubertin liked the idea, so the Greeks ran an Olympic trial that is believed to be the first marathon race, won in three hours eighteen minutes. Give me a time machine and a year of intense training, and I might have a shot at staying with the leaders in that one.

Pictures of the first Olympic marathon show men running in long pants along deserted roads. Spiridon Louis won in just under three hours – including a stop for a glass of wine. Consider that the first-ever aid station. Water, Gatorade or Cabernet Sauvignon?

After that first Olympic marathon of forty kilometres, the next six each had a different distance, ranging up to 42.75 kilometres. In the 1908 Olympic race in London, the starting line was moved so the Royal Family could have a better view, which pretty much sums up the priorities in Britain in 1908. The result was a race of 42.195 kilometres, which eventually became the standard distance.

If you've ever missed your marathon goal time by less than a minute, you can blame the British Royal Family for that extra 200 metres.

Marathon participation has had its ups and downs, but it seems to have settled into a new phase of sustainable growth.

In the 1960s and 1970s, small numbers of people started the first boom. In 1975, for example, 146 runners competed in the first Ottawa Marathon. You don't have to stare long at the photo from the starting line to know what decade it is: it's a sea of long hair, sideburns and beards, looking a bit like the gates just opened at a Grateful Dead concert.

The Ottawa Marathon peaked at 4,800 runners in 1983, but then fell on hard times. In the mid-'80s, stories from the archives refer to the end of the marathon-running "fad," and the race was officially cancelled in 1986.

But after a frenetic effort to attract investment, the 1986 race was resurrected with some 1,500 runners, plus a new ten-kilometre run held the night before the marathon.

At that time, race organizers across North America could only have dreamed of events featuring 40,000 participants or more. Maybe they got some help from Pan.

Now, as thousands every year continue a tradition that began with the fanciful legend of an Athenian herald, with help from a poet and a baron, only one question remains: Why didn't Pheidippides borrow a horse?

[**LOVE, HATE AND WINTER**]

iRun to enjoy all four seasons in Canada WAYNE SNOWDON, ONTARIO

I hate winter.

I hate the cold. I hate the snow and the slush. I hate the extra clothes you have to wear, the layers, the heavy boots. I hate shovelling and scraping. From Christmas until baseball season, I do whatever I can to avoid going outside. My main ambition in life is to find a way to be somewhere else for the first four months of every year. (So far, I have failed at my main ambition in life.)

Every winter, people close to me are subjected to six months of whining. During my regular shivery rants about winter, my father used to say, "But you're a Canadian." To which I would point out that I had no choice in being a Canadian, whereas he, born in a less wintry country, did. Then I would scowl, put on my parka and go home.

All of which make this fact all the more peculiar: I love winter running.

Learning this was as much a surprise to me as if I had suddenly discovered that I loved brussels sprouts. If, ten years ago, you took me in a time machine to see my future self jogging in minus -20C weather, I would have assumed that I had been sent to some kind of forced-labour camp.

Once upon a time, I was a fair-weather runner. If I managed

an outdoor run on one nice day in March, I thought I was being hardy. In the winter months, I exercised indoors, the way God intended.

Running on a treadmill was warmer than running outside, but I found it to be as boring as running in circles in your basement. If you think time is moving too quickly in your life, just get on a treadmill for half an hour. It's amazing how long even a minute can seem. I was constantly playing games with myself to avoid looking at the clock. Just stare straight ahead and don't look down for ten minutes, I would tell myself. Then I would run for what seemed like fifteen minutes, sneak a peek at the timer and find out it was only five.

When I started training for my first marathon, the long runs began in January. At first, I tried to figure out how I could do most of them indoors. The problem is that, at most gyms, you can't use a treadmill for more than thirty minutes at a time.

A few people said to me, try running outside, you'll love it. That's not possible, I said.

Having no other choice, though, I joined a running group to prepare for the marathon. I went shopping for winter running clothes. I bought a pair of running pants, a few long-sleeve shirts, a hat and something to cover my neck, mouth and nose. I now had the complete ensemble of a cat burglar. I learned, for the first time, about fabrics that "wick away" moisture. I learned that "wick" had another meaning unrelated to candles.

I started running with a friend in sub-zero temperatures. We did a couple of short early-morning runs when the temperature was minus -25, and another on a mid-January morning that was minus -30, with a windchill factor of minus -41.

What I learned very quickly was that I felt comfortable ten

minutes into the run, no matter how cold it was. The wind was sometimes frustrating, but the freezing temperatures stopped being an issue as soon as you were warmed up. I started to feel like I was tougher than I had thought, like I was withstanding winter conditions that normally made me cower.

A month later came the big test: a 26k group run on a Sunday morning with blowing snow and a windchill of minus -35. The wind was so strong that I was almost knocked over once or twice. My running partners and I were pelted with snow and ice. When I finished, I thought, if I can do this, I can do a marathon. Since then, I've become a committed year-round runner. I run as often in February as I do in August.

As someone once pointed out to me, there is no bad weather for running, only the wrong clothes. You have to adjust your pace sometimes and change your stride if it's slippery. You may also decide to take extra precautions, like making sure you have a cellphone or at least a quarter for a payphone. You don't want to get hurt ten kilometres from your house and have to hobble home in sub-zero temperatures.

I still prefer running in the spring and fall and early and late on hot summer days. But I've gone from being a fair-weather runner to being someone who sees the elements as a welcome challenge. After a winter run, I often get home with steam rising from my head and icicles on my earlobes and eyebrows, and feeling as though I've conquered the Canadian elements.

I've learned to love winter running, but I still hate winter.

[**BECAUSE IT'S THERE**]

iRun to paddle faster ADAM VAN KOEVERDEN, ONTARIO

I've asked a lot of people why they run. And our magazine has collected thousands of iRun statements in which people spell out what they love about running.

But this, from Olympic champion kayaker Adam van Koeverden, might just be the best answer I've ever heard:

"Why do I like running? Because it's there, I suppose. Because it's within my grasp. The same reason why I like doing everything that I do that's active: mountain-biking, kayaking, running, cross-country skiing. Because it's not going to get done if you don't do it."

Because it's there. If that's a sufficient excuse to attempt Mount Everest, as it was for George Mallory, it's a good enough reason to go for a run.

You know him as a kayaker, but van Koeverden is one of the most intensely passionate runners I've ever met. When we photographed him for a profile in *iRun* in the middle of winter, he insisted on doing an outdoor shot in which he would run through a cloud of snow. So I stood up to my knees in a snow bank and threw handfuls of snow in the air while photographer Colin Rowe captured van Koeverden sprinting through them.

How competitive is van Koeverden? Even though running is not his Olympic sport, all he wants to do is beat other runners.

"Whenever I see somebody in front of me, it doesn't matter how far away they are, I just love chasing them down," he says. "I don't care how fast they are, I want to get in front of them and pass them."

Van Koeverden started running before he started paddling. He ran cross-country in elementary school. And when he started kayaking, he noticed very few athletes at his club didn't run.

"Right away, I recognized that all the good kayakers in the world and all the good canoeists at my club and everybody I was training with were running quite a bit," he says. "You can't be on the water all the time as a kayaker with the weather in Canada. Running in the winter is a lot easier than breaking the ice to be in your kayak.

"I became a serious runner the day I became a serious kayaker."

How serious a runner? Despite having the physique of a kayaker, he came close to doing a seventeen-minute 5k in high school.

"For someone who was 185 pounds, that's pretty good. I remember lining up in cross-country in high school, looking over and thinking, 'These guys are 140.' I was pushing 190."

On top of his training in the kayak, van Koeverden ran three times a week at school, plus track workouts once a week. On Fridays, he would run twelve kilometres in the morning at school, then fourteen or fifteen at night with his canoe club.

"I'm glad I'm not doing it anymore because it's a lot of kilometres for a guy my weight," he says. "But it made me tough. It made me really tough."

Van Koeverden says he packs his running shoes wherever he goes. "Even if I'm going somewhere for a night, well, what if I wake up and want to go for a run? I can't leave these behind."

As an elite athlete with a finite career, he's already thinking ahead to life after kayaking, but he doesn't think he'll ever give up running.

"I will always be a runner. Running is just so accessible, I'll always do it. I'll always enjoy it and I'll always live somewhere close to trails and I can always just get on to the trail and give 'er in the trees for a few minutes.

"I always look forward to my next run. I could go on at length about the feeling you get after a run and the high that you feel and the sense of accomplishment that you get for days after. Even if you just did a short one, you just have something to reassure yourself that you're doing what you should be doing and getting the most out of your day."

Like many runners, van Koeverden dreams of running a marathon. But he wants to complete his Olympic career and then move down a weight class first. He's done a half-marathon in 1:18, so he figures he can break three hours in the marathon.

"I don't want to do a marathon until I'm sure I can crack three hours. I just don't want to run for three-and-a-half hours. I'd much rather run fast and be dead. But I'll have to lose some weight. Towards the end of a half-marathon, it's starting to hurt a lot in my joints."

Van Koeverden says he believes in getting the most out of every day, and he can't think of anything more productive that investing time in your health.

"From my perspective, the things that are worth enjoying are free. Running shoes aren't free, but it doesn't cost anything to get out there and go for a run."

[STUMBLING THROUGH THE WOODS]

iRun on instinct IAN PERRIMAN, BRITISH COLUMBIA

It seems I have weak ankles. At least that's what I concluded from an otherwise satisfying and glorious trail run through the woods early one morning a few years ago.

I had never been much of a trail runner. I usually found myself spending a lot of time looking down, watching for roots and rocks, instead of taking in what was around me. For me, the uneven terrain was extra work and extra stress; preventing me from getting into a good rhythm. You struggle up a short hill and then try to fight the gravity going down the other side. You go up and down, sideways, turn left, turn right, over logs, dodging rocks, stepping between tree roots, avoiding puddles and mud. So you never relax, never settle into the groove of a good long road run.

But those kinds of challenges constitute a healthy break from the monotony of running the same route through your neighbourhood.

An invitation from an old friend to run through the autumn leaves was too much to resist. Which is why I was up at six o'clock on a Saturday morning, driving through the dark to rural Quebec. The plan was for three men and a dog to take a two-hour run through the woods.

We started out just as the day was breaking. It was a morning to savour: clear and crisp and just below zero. At any time, this would be a spectacular route, but in autumn, it was even more special. We were basically running on an enormous bed of leaves. It made the trail less evident, but thankfully my friend had run it many times. The sky was perfect, the temperature ideal and I was quickly warmed up and enjoying a comfortable pace.

The challenges of the route made the time move more quickly. Another benefit of trail running is a relief from the pounding of a road or bike path. In autumn, the leaves can make for an especially soft landing. But what lies beneath can pose problems; the leaves are a clever disguise for rocks, roots and soft spots, and this quickly became a problem.

My experience from a few previous trail runs was that if I don't land with a flat foot, I can easily stumble or turn an ankle. With alarming regularity on this run, I found myself recovering from minor stumbles. I found it particularly common when I was running downhill. I would stretch a little bit to get over a root or a branch lying across the path and when I landed on something unexpected, with the force of my stride plus a little extra gravity, I paid a price. I ended up on the side of my foot, feeling a sharp pain in the ankle, plus a little shot of adrenaline and a jump in my heart rate.

What you fear most is an injury – a sprain or worse – that will sideline you for weeks. You lurch to the side, almost wipe out completely, then regain your balance and hobble for two or three steps. And then it becomes clear that the pain is passing and no major damage has been done.

For some reason, this seemed to happen to me about four times as often as for my two running partners. They were both almost as good as our four-legged companion at navigating the terrain.

After it happened a few times, it became harder to stay relaxed; unfortunately, that apprehension can make it more likely to happen again. If you're tense, you don't react as fluidly. When it happens a few times in the space of a few hundred metres, it can become very frustrating.

But that didn't overshadow the benefits. Here I am, I thought, a few minutes and an eternity from my home, drawing in clean air and working up a comfortable sweat, and with good company.

After a while, as on any long run, the conversation gave way to a comfortable silence. The sun was peeking through the trees as it rose over the hills, illuminating the wet terrain. The leaves beneath our feet changed from a mixture of yellow, green and brown to a brighter combination of reds and purples. It was as peaceful as anything involving exertion can be. A rhythm settled in and there was only the gentle sound of feet on leaves, the occasional twig breaking.

Until I disturbed the calm by stumbling once more.

[**FASTER, HARDER**]

iRun to challenge my perceived limitations CASSANDRA WILLIAMS, ONTARIO

When I ran my first marathon, I went deliberately slow. I was less concerned about finishing time than finishing at all. And I knew that if I fed any hint of a time goal to my compulsive, competitive personality, I would risk going too fast.

So I avoided the temptation of aiming for a sub-four-hour finish, trained with a 4:15 pace group and finished in about 4:08.

That gave me an obvious goal for my next marathon, which I planned to do the following spring: to break four hours. But in between, I decided to run a fall half-marathon and use it as a test of whether I had the capacity to go a bit faster.

I'd only run one half-marathon before. Using the same principle of avoiding a time goal, I finished in about 2:03. So for this next test, I figured anything under two hours would be an improvement. I joined the 1:50 pace group at a clinic and started working towards a specific finishing time for the first time in my life.

I figured if I trained for 1:50, I would have a bit of room to spare. Even if things didn't go well, I could still break two hours.

At this point in my life, one of the things I liked about running was that I wasn't very good at it. It's rewarding to find out that you excel at something, and it's fun and enriching to be a leader and carry some responsibility. But I discovered one of the reasons I liked running, at least at first, was because I didn't feel any pressure to be the best or run at the front of the pack.

I run my own business. On family trips, I'm usually both the driver and the navigator. I'm a little competitive, so I feel the urge to win whether I'm at work, participating in a recreational sport or even playing board games with kids. I had a pretty good winning streak going in Horse-opoly before my wife pointed out that it might not be healthy for my step-daughter to lose every game.

But in my first marathon clinic, I was happy to fall in behind other more experienced runners during training runs. I was glad to be a follower and not a leader. There's a lot less pressure in the middle of the pack.

As I was training for this half-marathon in particular, I felt especially happy to fall in line behind other runners. My father's health was deteriorating and I found running my only diversion from confronting the fact that he would soon be gone.

So when they asked for volunteers to lead the 1:50 pace group, I started looking at my feet. Unfortunately, the store manager was a friend, and when no one else put up a hand, he singled me out.

I told Jen, the clinic leader, that it felt wrong to be leading a pace group at a speed I had never run before. She reassured me that I would be fine. Besides, there was no one else to do it. I wasn't even sure I could break two hours in a half-marathon and now I was leading the pace group that was supposed to go ten minutes faster than that.

I have a hard time saying no, so for the next few months, I led a small group of runners on their weekly long run. It went better than I expected. In fact, one day one of them gently complained that we were going too fast. Jen just happened to be nearby so she asked,

"Still worried you can't run fast enough?"

Maybe it was because after slogging through the winter training for a marathon, this time we were training during the summer for a fall event. Maybe it's because I was a group leader and had no choice but to talk to the other runners. Either way, I discovered that I was enjoying the social aspect of the clinic a lot more. I got to know several of the runners and our runs together became something I looked forward to every week. My life consisted of going to work, visiting my father at his hospice and going for a run.

About ten days before the race, my father died. After the funeral, I decided there was no reason for me not to run the race I'd been training for. My aunt, who travelled from England for the funeral, offered to come out and cheer me on.

I told myself I would be very happy with anything between 1:50 and 1:55 and certainly wouldn't be disappointed as long as I finished under two hours. But to my surprise, I managed to sustain a steady pace and finished in just over 1:44, much faster than I ever expected. Jen was right to believe I could go faster than I thought I could.

Not surprisingly, I liked the feeling of hitting a time goal and exceeding my expectations. It's good to aim low to avoid the risk of disappointment. And there's nothing wrong with trying not to put too much pressure on your running, especially if you've got other pressures in life.

But you also shouldn't avoid the chance to live up to your potential. I'm glad I was pushed into running harder. It gave me the chance to surprise myself and the incentive to try to go even faster in the future.

[THE BEER MILE]

iRun for beer DARYLL SMITH, ONTARIO

Canadian runners are not the favourites to win the Olympic marathon. No Canadian has won the Boston Marathon in a quarter of a century. And no Canadian has ever been the holder of the fastest recorded time in the mile.

But one Canadian runner has a stranglehold on the world record in another event: the Beer Mile.

What's the Beer Mile? It's as simple as this: A mile is roughly four laps of a standard 400-metre track. In the Beer Mile, you drink a can of beer before each lap. Four beers, four laps.

And Jim Finlayson, a two-time Canadian marathon champion, has done it faster than anyone in the world. You know the once-elusive four-minute mile? Finlayson, of Victoria, B.C., is closing in on the five-minute Beer Mile. Finlayson's world record performance of 5:09 is more than half-a-minute faster than anyone else.

I know this for a fact: I couldn't do one or the other in that time. Running a mile or drinking four beers would take me a lot longer than five minutes. Finlayson can do both. Not bad for a guy who stumbled upon the event only a couple of years before his world-record performance.

In 2005, Finlayson entered the Dave Smart Tribute Beer Mile, a fundraiser for a foundation named in honour of a Victoria triathlete who died at thirty-three of melanoma.

"I had no idea what to expect," says Finlayson. "I entered for fun and I figured I would just go as hard as I could and see how it turned out."

It turned out very well. Finlayson finished first with a time of 5:13, much faster than the world record of 5:40. But he drank his favourite beer, Guinness, which has a lower alcohol content than allowed in the rules, so his time wasn't official.

(Yes, there are some very specific rules for the Beer Mile. Basically anything you can think of that would make it easier to chug beer when you're out of breath – everything from light beer to wide-mouth bottles to shot-gunning – is prohibited. Oh, and you have to bring all the beer with you to the finish line. If you throw up, you run a penalty lap.)

"I was surprised at how well I was able to adapt to both parts of the race," says Finlayson.

Event organizers encouraged him to race again the next year with an approved beer so that a world record could be set. But he didn't decide to enter until the day of the race.

"I wasn't planning on doing it," he says. "But then I just couldn't not give it a try." So he stopped by the liquor store and picked up a six-pack.

"I asked the guy in the store, 'What's the closest thing to Guinness that has five per cent alcohol?' He gave me Keeper's Stout. I found it pretty fizzy, but it counted."

Finlayson finished in 5:20 and set a new record.

In December 2007, he started thinking about another attempt.

"Two weeks before the race, I was really excited about it. But then I started having second thoughts. I was actually getting a bit nervous. What if it goes horribly wrong this year?"

Once again, it was a last-minute decision. After a practice run the night before with a new drink – Granville Island Winter Ale – Finlayson broke his own record in front of a field of more than seventy-five runners and a boisterous crowd of about a hundred people.

Finlayson says he'd like to take a crack at breaking five minutes. But even so, he has mixed feelings about being the world's fastest Beer Miler.

"I feel good and I feel embarrassed at the same time," he says. "There's definitely some pride there. But having that beer label attached to it, I'm not really sure how I should feel about it. Sometimes I feel that as runners, we should be leading this clean lifestyle, but you can be an athlete and still enjoy a beer."

Sometimes you can even do both at the same time.

[**THE AGELESS RUNNER**]

iRun because I want to grow old gracefully AIMEE SMITH, ONTARIO

Imagine running a half-marathon on your fifty-seventh wedding anniversary. You'd probably be glad just to be running when you've been married for half a century, let alone put in 21.1k.

Now, pretend for a second that you only did the half because you'd already run three marathons in the last six months.

Now you're starting to get a sense of the astonishing accomplishments of Betty Jean McHugh, the octogenarian marvel from North Vancouver, B.C.

McHugh doesn't just defy aging, she's declared it obsolete. She runs four times a week – usually at 5:45 a.m. Some of the women she runs with are half her age (of course, it's not like she could find five other eighty-year-olds to run with). She does hills and speedwork and, when she's not running, cycles for cross-training, practises yoga and hits the gym for strength training.

Along the way, she's picked up more than a dozen Canadian and world records, including the fastest-ever marathons for women aged seventy-five and eighty.

Show me another grandmother who would say, as she was about to travel with her kids to Rome to run the marathon, "It will be such a lovely family outing." Or who would decide, after running a marathon about once every two years, to start doing them more often because "I figured I was running out of years."

But it wasn't always this way. McHugh didn't even start running until she was fifty-five. While her daughter, who went on to swim for Canada at the 1972 Olympics, was training at the pool, McHugh ran along the beach in her tennis shoes. She joined a fitness club, ran a 10k and then did her first marathon and finished in 3:32.

"I thought, 'I'll never do another one. I just have to get it out of my system.'"

But she, like so many other runners who have said the same thing, was hooked. She started doing destination marathons in places like London and Honolulu. She trained with a group of runners who spurred her on to keep racing. They talked her into running a marathon when she turned 75, and she set a world record.

In October 2008, running in Victoria, she chopped thirteen minutes off the record for eighty-year-old women. Then she ran Honolulu a couple of months later.

"She is something else," says Heather Parker, who runs with McHugh. "My body's not holding up as well as B.J.'s and I'm only sixty-two."

Parker marvels at McHugh's attitude and her approach not just to running, but to life. "She never complains. She's bright and cheery and positive. She has a big breakfast every morning. She likes to read an hour a day. She makes everything from scratch."

Yet in spite of her success and longevity, McHugh doesn't even seem to realize what an inspiring story she's become.

"I don't actually think about it that much," she says. "I don't like all the hubbub about it." So when race officials in Rome contacted her offering a free trip to Italy to run the marathon, she thought it was a joke and never replied.

"Someone wrote to me and said, 'I want you to run the Rome Marathon, all expenses paid.' I thought, 'Who would want to do that?' So I let it ride."

Luckily, they were persistent. When she got there, organizers treated McHugh like an elite athlete.

"Rome was awesome," she says. "In all my life, next to being born, I think it was the next best thing I've ever done.

"The best part of the whole thing was that I felt so privileged to be up front with all these Kenyans. They insisted I run as an elite runner. This is the icing on the cake of my career."

And she's not done yet. There are plans to run more marathons. It's up to the group, McHugh says. Without them, she figures she wouldn't still be racing.

"They are so good to me. I wouldn't be doing this if it wasn't for them."

But there has to be something more to it than that. True to her humble form, McHugh says it's just a bit of luck.

"It's probably genetics," she says. "I've been blessed with good health and good joints."

[COMPETING AGAINST YOURSELF]

iRun to run my own race COLLEEN SHEPPARD, ONTARIO

When you compete in a race, who are you really racing against? At the New York City Marathon, it's thousands of other athletes. At smaller events, it might be fewer than 200.

But are you racing against those other runners or racing with them? For a handful of people who have a shot at winning, it really is a competitive race with real opponents. And I suppose if your archrival is in the same event and you want to be waiting for him at the finish line with a satisfied look on your face, you may believe it's a true contest.

If you're the typical runner, though, you are competing against only one person: yourself.

While to some people that might sound like a cliché you'd throw at your kid to teach him sportsmanship, it's the prime motivation for most runners.

It's not that they aren't competitive, but most have shifted those instincts away from others and toward themselves.

Sure, you can look at someone who can do a 2:30 marathon and wish you could go that fast. But one thing that appeals to me about running is that far from being your opponents, the people around you are a source of inspiration and encouragement.

Whenever I've been training, I've met many athletes who are

all working toward largely the same personal goal: to go farther or faster. I've met people who are trying to qualify for the Boston Marathon. I've heard stories about people who didn't finish their first attempt at a marathon and are training hard to try again.

If you're like most runners, the toughest and most worthy competitor you'll ever face is yourself. And when you go farther or faster than you ever have before, that's more satisfying than beating any other opponent.

That's why so many runners talk regularly about their personal best times, or "PBs." The PB reflects the peak of your own performance, and a standard you may still be trying to beat. Most athletes know their own by heart, down to the second.

In 2004, I finished a half-marathon in just over an hour and forty-four minutes. I was hoping to break 1:50, so I was pretty happy with that.

On training runs, I still picture myself breaking the tape at the finish line of an important long-distance race, to the shock of Kenyans far behind me, but I've accepted the fact that outside of my dreams, I may never even qualify for Boston.

But if you test the limits of your abilities, you might find that although you're in the middle or back of the pack, you may be faster than you thought. That's what happened to me when I started training a little more intensely in 2006. I started running shorter distances at speeds that suggested I had the potential to do better times in my longer races.

Of course, all those indicators mean nothing once the race starts, which is why I was a little nervous before running the a half-marathon in which I hoped to set a new personal best. I was aiming to finish in just under 1:40. But to maintain that speed over 21.1 kilometres still seemed impossible to me.

Thankfully, the weather co-operated. I stuck to my race plan of maintaining a steady pace of 4:45 per kilometre, avoiding the temptation to speed up to catch friends who were ahead of me.

All race, I felt right on the edge between comfort and pain, as if I was pushing myself, but not so hard that it would cost me in the final few kilometres. I was right where I wanted to be.

I tried to avoid looking at my watch too often, in case it had bad news for me, or such good news that I might start to worry about burning out.

With half a kilometre to go, I saw my coach, Rick Hellard, on the sidelines. Rick had already won the race in 1:13 and was wandering back up the course. He looked at his watch.

"You're under 1:37," he said as I ran past. "You've got lots of time. You're going to get a PB!"

Just what I needed to hear. I felt a surge of energy and picked up the pace. In the final 200 metres, I could see the clock ahead of me: 1:39:35 ... 1:39:36 ... 1:39:37. I started sprinting, surprised that I had some excess energy left this late in the race. I crossed the finish line at 1:39:51. My actual time from start to finish, which takes into account that I was at the back of the pack when the gun went off, was 1:39:17.

I hit my goal with more than forty seconds to spare. I beat my previous best time by more than five minutes. I outdid my biggest rival: my younger self.

[WHY RACING BEATS EVERYDAY LIFE]

iRun for the pure enjoyment of racing MIKE WHITE, ONTARIO

For the amateur runner, nothing beats the race experience. In a race, you are the focus of attention, just like the elite competitors. That's why, even though they can be gruelling and don't always go as well as planned, races are way better than everyday life.

Don't think so? Then tell me when any of these things ever happen to you on a regular day.

When you wander through the hallways at the office, do people clap as you go past? Or ring bells?

When you're doing your everyday job, do members of your family gather to watch you and shout encouragement? Do they make signs with markers and bristol board that say, "Go Heather!" or "You can do it"? Do your friends in other countries monitor your progress online and send you congratulatory e-mails?

Is there a rock band or brass quartet playing upbeat music on the side of the road when you drive downtown? Or belly dancers? (OK, that's probably a good thing.)

When you make your way through a busy day, is there a table with refreshments on it at regular intervals, where volunteers are just waiting for you to arrive so they can hand you the drink of your choice as you zip past without stopping?

When you're walking around your neighbourhood, is it

considered acceptable for you to throw your cup on the ground when you're finished with it and expect someone to rush over, pick it up and throw it out for you?

At the end of a long meeting, is there a room with free bagels and neatly cut-up bananas and orange wedges waiting for you, to replenish you and reward you for surviving the ordeal?

When you're driving down the road and you pass someone, do they wish you luck as you go by?

When you're working outside on a hot day, does anyone ever give you a sponge so that you can squeeze water over your head and instantly cool off?

When you're strolling through the mall, do you expect that by wearing a shirt with your name on it, there will be complete strangers calling out, "Good job, Rhonda!" or "Go, Bob!"?

Does the city ever close a series of major roads for you and station police officers along the route so that you can get where you need to go without vehicles getting in the way?

When you're trying to find your way around an unfamiliar area, are there volunteers standing there, waiting for you, so they can wave you in the right direction?

Is there a website you can go to that shows you how everything in the rest of your life – your investment portfolio, your cooking skills, your sense of humour – stacks up against other people in your age group?

When you complete a work-related project, or a task around the house, is there any bling? Does anybody put a medal around your neck and congratulate you, even if you didn't finish on time or perform particularly well? Is there an announcer calling out your name and imploring people to cheer for you?

How often in your life when you are not running a race are there people yelling out, "You're looking good!" or "Nice legs!"?

When you're in the final stages of mowing the lawn or doing the laundry, does anybody ever try to give you a last-minute surge of energy by calling out, "You're almost there!"?

When you finished building that shed in your backyard, did someone come up beside you and put a foil cape around your shoulders and treat you like a hero that had just returned from battle?

Name another circumstance where a complete stranger will high-five you. Or let his kid do the same.

Unless you're the mayor, is there any other circumstance in your life when there are official photographers positioned strategically to record special moments and then provide you with a selection of photos afterward?

When you get back from a gruelling day of appointments, can you just stop in to the massage tent and get a free rubdown? Does your spouse draw a warm bath for you when you get home?

I didn't think so.

[PEOPLE OF AUDACIOUS HOPE]

iRun to dream big MARK COLLIS, ONTARIO

It starts with the note.

The note was handwritten by a teenage girl inspired by the Montreal Olympics. It was dated September 11, 1976, and then carefully concealed, tucked under a couple of loose floorboards in the bedroom of an old farmhouse in rural Ontario.

It was simply too audacious to be shared. So there the note stayed, year after year. Not even the girl who wrote it dared to dig it out, not even to scan it briefly and reaffirm the handful of words, lest the hiding place be discovered.

When the girl's mother stumbled upon the note, she replaced it carefully and left it there, untouched for another decade. Not a word was spoken about it.

The note is simple enough. In one sentence, two goals are set. And even though one of them was never met – perhaps especially so – in that note a determination was established, a character was defined, one that would outlast either objective and serve the writer for a lifetime.

The note belonged to Silvia Ruegger, and it plainly set out her goal of going to the Olympics and winning a medal for Canada. And in 1984, she ran in the first Olympic women's marathon, setting a Canadian record and finishing eighth. Though she tried for three more Olympiads, and along the way set a new Canadian marathon record that still stands today, she never returned to the Games to win a medal. But the journey taught her a lesson she was determined to share.

"One of my favourite quotes is, 'The highest reward for a person's toil is not what he or she gets for it but what he or she becomes by it,'" says Ruegger. "If you believe that ultimately the most lasting and richest rewards are in the journey, it allows you to keep going without worrying about what happens."

That's what pushed Ruegger to keep training, in spite of a serious accident and a series of injuries, until 1996.

"Some people would say, wasn't that a waste," she says. "You spent twelve years of your life pursuing a goal and it didn't work.

"But it's the journey. We have to persevere. It gives us the opportunity to inspire others. We become people of audacious hope. It forever changes our perspective on life. What we thought was impossible before we see as possible."

That audacious hope not only motivated Ruegger to speak to runners, especially women, it inspired her to launch a program for disadvantaged young children. There are now KidsFit Running and Reading after-school clubs across Canada, where children read books and train for a 5k.

Looking back on her Olympic experience, Ruegger has nothing but pride.

"I have never forgotten the incredible honour and privilege it was to participate in that event, to be in that historic event with pioneers in the sport, to wear that Canadian jacket.

There's a lot of gratitude. What I really appreciate is that the walls and barriers came down at the right time for me.

"You carry a responsibility because you know you're

representing your nation. It's a privilege, but it's also a responsibility. I definitely remember that feeling."

Interestingly, before running the first Olympic women's marathon in Los Angeles in 1984, Ruegger had run only one marathon: the Canadian Olympic qualifying event a few months earlier in Ottawa. But she didn't feel under-prepared for the distance. Unlike a runner following a conventional marathon training plan, Ruegger actually ran the full marathon distance – and beyond – several times in the lead up to the race.

"We would actually go beyond the marathon distance," she says. "We would go thirty miles (48k) in training. And at the twenty-six-mile mark (42k) we would drop our training pace to race pace. At the point at which you would think, 'now we're done,' it's 'no you're not, you're going to go even harder.'

"Even though the Olympic Games was only my second marathon, I had experienced what it was going to be like in each of those situations. So you're not surprised by anything."

Since her historic event, Ruegger has watched women's distance running evolve dramatically.

"I'm thrilled with how far it's come. The change has been quite dramatic and quite quick since 1984. When I speak to women, it's amazing how many of them say 'Really?' when I say the first Olympic women's marathon was in 1984.

"I'm thrilled with seeing women of all ages now engaged in the sport. I know the power of sport in terms of what it can do in your life. There are just so many life lessons you get from running. That's what excites me about seeing women involved in sports. It changes their perspective on a lot of things. Things before that they didn't think they could do, they now think they can do.

"All of a sudden they see themselves as a runner, a marathoner or someone who can finish a 5k. It changes their perspective on what they can do. I tell them: "You can do it. You do have what it takes."

Ruegger's outlook, her faith, is that in running and in life, the journey has infinite rewards.

"Running is about putting one step in front of the other," she says, "but it's about a whole lot more than that. The journey is incredibly rewarding. Before you even get to that starting line, the rewards are already yours."

$$\left[\text{ FINISHED AT THE FINISH } \right]$$

iRun to find my limits MARK GIDDENS, ONTARIO

This is not the graceful finish I planned.

I have suddenly found myself sitting on the ground some three metres past the finish line. Other runners are zooming past on either side of me, still on their feet. A young volunteer in a red shirt is beside me in an instant. I think he had a colleague with him who was pushing an empty wheelchair.

"Let's get you back on your feet," he says. "Can you walk?"

"Yes," I say boldly, although I'm not sure.

I have some energy left, but my muscles are shot. Which is, I suppose, how you want them to be at the end of a marathon. Leave everything on the course, the saying goes. Only now it's me that's on the course. Better a few metres after the finish line than anywhere before it.

With about two kilometres left to run in a marathon in 2006, I started feeling occasional little shots of pain – maybe a cramping feeling, it was hard to tell – in my calves. With about 500 metres to go, I was feeling it on every step. It's the kind of pain that warns you off putting weight on that leg. Only it was in both legs and I was trying to finish a marathon.

I managed to fight it off, and I think even speed up a bit, in the final 200 metres. But two steps after the finish line, my right leg gave way and I started to tumble. I managed to turn around as I was falling so that instead of doing a face plant, I just sat down rather inelegantly. In the middle of the finish line.

"I'll walk with you for a while," says the man in the red shirt. So off we go, each with an arm around the other's shoulder.

"I'm OK now," I say.

"Let's just make sure," he says, and we go a little further together, my new best friend and I.

It was kind of an odd coincidence to find myself in this situation. For some last-minute inspiration, on the night before the race I stood at the finish line of the 10k event, where I watched some remarkable runners complete their runs. But I also saw a handful of people take finish-line tumbles. One or two had to be carried across the line and then whisked away in wheelchairs. Given the heat Saturday night and the similar forecast for Sunday morning, I wondered if a similar fate awaited me.

The weather was actually an enormous factor in the race. After all those cloudy and rainy weekends when I prayed for sunshine, this was the one weekend I was hoping it wouldn't be sunny and warm. Mother Nature has what the French call an *esprit de contradiction*.

The first half of the marathon was pleasant enough. But when I reached the wide-open road that made up much of the second half, I was in for twenty kilometres of running in the bright sunshine, with the temperature climbing and the heat rising off the pavement. For the last nine kilometres, I was in a constant battle with myself not to stop running.

My goal was to finish in as close as possible to three hours and thirty minutes. I was on pace, give or take a minute, through thirty-two kilometres. Experts say this is the point at which the marathon really begins. In my case, it was when I began to slow down. I finished in 3:38:46; considering the heat and the fact that it's a thirteen-minute improvement on my previous best time, I was thrilled.

But I was also afraid to take off my shoes.

I wasn't ready to confront my feet. There was a strong likelihood of blistering on the ball of my right foot. I started feeling that about halfway through the race. And I was feeling pain around a toenail on my left foot, which meant I could have the dreaded purple nail.

My friendly finish-line volunteer – I never got his name – sent me on my way after about fifty metres. "Congrats," he said, and then he was off to help someone else.

As comical as my finish-line tumble was, I'm looking at it as a good sign. On that day, in that heat, I did the best I possibly could. I barely had a step left in me after 42.2 kilometres.

[ONE DAY AFTER ANOTHER]

iRun because it has been a habit for thirty-five years PETER HUNT, ALBERTA

The story of Rick Rayman's inconceivable running record begins on a day when he didn't go running. It was December 9, 1978.

At the time, Rayman was pretty new to running, but he had embraced it with a passion. He ran every day. For about five months leading up to December 9, Rayman hadn't missed a single day.

But that day, he simply didn't feel like it.

"We were coming home from a family vacation in Florida," says Rayman. "I was with my wife and kids for two straight weeks. And I realized, 'I gotta go back to work tomorrow.' I was so depressed. And I just didn't run."

He got over it quickly. Rayman ran the next day. And he's run every single day since.

For more than thirty-two years, more than 11,000 straight days, Rick Rayman has run. And run. And run.

All for one simple reason. "I just love doing it," he says.

He doesn't just stick to a simple 5k every day. Over the years, Rayman has run more than 200 marathons. In some years, he runs as many as eighteen of them, including marathons on six consecutive weekends. Not bad for a guy who still works in his own dental practice and teaches dentistry at the University of Toronto.

Since he started his career as a dentist in Toronto in 1970, Rayman has missed only three days of work. But even on those days, he still managed to run.

"A few years ago, I had a terrible, terrible cold and upper respiratory infection, so I missed work on Monday and Tuesday," he says. "But I still got out of bed and went out for a thirty-minute run.

"I went out for thirty minutes, came back, showered, shaved and got back into bed."

Even after a marathon, Rayman doesn't take a day off to recover.

"I'm a little tired when I go to work on Monday mornings," he says. "I've rearranged my Mondays so I get to work at ten o'clock."

So, rather than take the day off, he takes an hour or two off.

Rayman used to run fast. Through hard training, he got his marathon time down to as low as 2:47. And when he started slowing down, at first he didn't like it.

"When I ran a 3:01, I was totally distressed," he says.

But then something surprising happened – running slower actually rejuvenated his interest in the sport. "I started running a different type of marathon," he says. "And we met a whole new breed of runners."

Running in Virginia Beach one March, Rayman had a hamstring injury and ended up walking most of the second half of the race. "I finished in six hours, but I didn't care," he says. The group of runners and walkers he finished with inspired him to keep going. "It was a whole different type of person out there. People were cheering for them and they were all smiling and everyone was happy."

It helps, of course, that Rayman has a patient wife, Martha, who travels with him to almost all of his races. He and Martha have embraced the lifestyle of the travelling runner: the long drives, the expos, the crowds.

"I love this," he says. "It sounds corny but I love it. I love the people. I love the everyday runner. I just love being around runners."

If running eighteen marathons in one year sounds crazy to you, Rayman figures there's another level of insanity. He knows runners who do more than twice that many, sometimes two marathons the same weekend.

"I don't know how these people run forty marathons a year," he says. "I don't know how they afford it. It's expensive."

So what goal does a man set when he's run more than 200 marathons? What do you aspire to when you've run every day for three decades?

"I want to run more," says Rayman. "My goal is just to keep on doing it. That's it."

[RUNNING THE GLOBE]

Is there another sport more portable than running? As Adam van Koeverden pointed out, you can throw a pair of shoes in your suitcase and run anywhere in the world. Try bringing your canoe to Chicago or finding a squash partner or a pickup hockey game in Europe.

It helps when you remember the shoes. Not long ago, I had a cunning plan to save space in my suitcase by wearing my brand-new running shoes on the plane. I was at the airport before I realized I had defaulted to my everyday shoes in the rush to get out the door for the taxi. So I had to buy a second pair of new shoes when I got to Florida.

Some of my favourite runs have happened on the familiar ground of my hometown routes. Simple math dictates that many of my best memories would come from the roads most travelled. But a disproportionate number of memorable runs have happened hundreds or even thousands of kilometres from home.

I'm not a constant traveller, but over the last decade, I've run up and down the English dales and through Quebec's cottage country, under the Eiffel Tower and over the Brooklyn Bridge, across Canadian cities from Charlottetown to Edmonton, through the rich neighbourhoods of Buenos Aires and Boston, on the islands of Cape Breton and the Caribbean, on the beaches of Florida's Gulf Coast to Uruguay's Punta del Este.

When I'm not training for a specific event, I enjoy the opportunity to take a run through a new city and get to know it more intimately than if I was just a tourist in a cab, heading straight to a specific destination. Runs are a chance to acclimatize, get your bearings and explore (and justify a few extra vacation calories).

When I'm at a conference or out of town for meetings, I relish the chance to get up before everyone else and getting in my run before the day's busy schedule begins. I love the feeling of going down to breakfast and feeling awake and alive because I've already had a great run, while many others are trying to wake up by injecting themselves with coffee.

And when I'm training for a race, I look forward to the challenge of integrating long runs into my journeys. What could be better than mapping out a twenty-five-kilometre route in a new location? It beats running the same course every weekend back home. Besides, you'll see places you never would have as an ordinary visitor.

In 2009, while training for a fall marathon, I set off from my cousin's house in Yorkshire and ran about sixteen kilometres along a little-used path by the River Calder to a place called Sowerby Bridge, then back home again. Running on my own through unfamiliar territory was a test of endurance and perseverance. It was tranquil, scenic and spectacular, and one of the highlights of my trip. And when I got back, most people were just getting out of bed.

A couple of years earlier, I left my hotel room before dawn and ran up and down the hill to Edinburgh Castle. The city was just waking up and I felt like I had it all to myself. Let's just say the hill runs I do in my neighbourhood don't culminate at a historic landmark from the twelfth century.

In 2006, while visiting friends in Buenos Aires, I found a neighbourhood street that was 400 metres long and ran a series of intervals from one end to the other. A shopkeeper who poked her head out the window a few times must have wondered why I passed so often.

In 2010, I left my hotel in the 5eme arrondissement of Paris and ran along the Seine to the Eiffel Tower, where I saw the sun rise and light up the steel structure. I'll remember that run for a long time.

A few days before my wedding in 2008, I ran the Trans Canada Trail in Charlottetown and finished just after passing the P.E.I. legislature. A few days later, I ran ten kilometres on the reddest dirt road I've ever seen.

For several summers, when my friend Bob has spent weekends at his cottage, I've driven up to join him for long runs in the woods and on the highways of Western Quebec. There is nothing better than jumping into a lake after a hilly run on a hot sunny day.

And when my family rented a cottage in the same area in 2010, I had a 32k run to complete, in preparation for another fall marathon. I set off early and ran two giant loops on my own, stopping back at the cottage for water at the midway point. Along the way, with nothing but lots of road ahead of me, I mapped out the plot of a novel I'll probably never write.

On every run away from home, I've felt a sense of discovery and excitement and the challenge of covering unfamiliar ground. None of which I would get in a hotel gym.

[JUST LIKE US]

iRun to find out what I'm made of DANA MORGAN, BRITISH COLUMBIA

My favourite section from the trashy gossip magazines appears in *Us Weekly*, where every issue they point out the following fact: "Stars – They're Just Like Us." Choosing to ignore the rather large gap in income, home size and plastic-surgery bill between the average reader and your typical Hollywood celebrity, the magazine proves through a series of pictures that famous actors and singers walk their dogs, plug the parking meter and purchase fruit – just like us!

At the risk of sounding just as inane, I now reveal the following piece of information: famous people who run are just like other runners. They lace up their shoes just like us. They struggle with the same training challenges. And they get pleasure and pain out of the sport, just like us.

Running is one of life's greatest common denominators. When I joined a clinic a few years ago, I ran with the same group of people every Sunday for two months without learning any of their surnames. We talked for hours at a time and shared intimate details about our personal lives. But I didn't find out one of them was a doctor until months after our race, when I ran into him in a completely different context.

Two people who might otherwise never even cross paths,

much less have anything to talk about, can be brought together by a simple activity and a goal of staying in shape or finishing a particular race. Even if they never run together, they can share running with each other.

Which is how I've come to be trading running stories with dozens of well-known Canadians: Olympic champions, hockey stars, politicians and television personalities.

I especially enjoyed hearing some of them talk about running in far-off places. Many people have run on the deck of a cruise ship, but CBC journalist Evan Solomon ran on board a Canadian frigate in the Persian Gulf.

"We got up at six o'clock with the elite boarding crew and we jogged around the helicopter deck," he said. "It's 6:00 a.m., you're in the Persian Gulf, forty kilometres off the coast of Iran, and you're jogging."

Even though what happens in Las Vegas is supposed to stay there, Solomon also shared a story of a run down the strip at 7:30 a.m.

"I'm like the only guy there," he said. "People are still gambling and I'm jogging the strip. They look at me like I'm the biggest nerd in history. What are you doing in Las Vegas jogging? It's the place where you do everything but that."

Federal cabinet minister Stockwell Day told me of a spectacular run in China. "Running from a hotel in Beijing down through the streets to Tiananmen Square early in the morning was a pretty amazing experience."

His cabinet colleague Peter MacKay has run everywhere from Argentina to Vietnam. He did laps of the Canadian military base in Afghanistan, where he says dust got into every pore of his body. And he described the unique experience of running as a visiting dignitary, where a support crew is provided by the host country.

"They usually put security on you," he says. "I had one very funny experience in Rome. They assigned these two middle-age overweight heavy smokers. I started to jog and they were coming behind me in street shoes. I said, 'I'm going to go around the park. You wait here.' They said that was okay as long as I didn't tell their superior officer."

Canadian General Andrew Leslie has run during military postings in such places as Bosnia and Cyprus. But he remembers one particular run in a region where the situation was getting dire.

"I guess the most memorable run would have been my time in Croatia just before a small war broke out," he said. "So as we're running, you could hear shellfire fifteen or twenty kilometres away. We were in no immediate danger, but it created a surreal background in which to go for a fitness run."

Solomon and Day share a love of the morning run, partly because it's the only time of the day they can be sure to fit it into their busy lives.

"You see the mist, you see the day begin," said Solomon. "In the winter it's dark. You see all the seasons at that time of the day. When you have kids, you suddenly realize how amazing solitude is. It becomes a really important part of the day to be that quiet, to be that alone. When I run alone, it's a totally different experience than running with a friend."

"There's something about early mornings," said Day. "They're always kind of special. Beautiful mornings are good. And if you get a wind with sleet in your eyes, it gives you a sense that you're paying the price and you come away feeling like you've challenged the elements and won – whether you're running a two-kilometre run early in the morning or whether you're running twenty kilometres."

Whether a runner is famous or not, I like hearing about the role that running plays in his or her life. Technology journalist and social-media sensation Amber MacArthur talked about training for a marathon after the end of a long-term relationship. "It was four months of therapy to get over a guy," she said. "It's probably a fairly common reason."

MacKay says he runs to clear his mind. "It's a great release. It allows you to rid your body of a lot of the tension. It helps me untangle things on my mind. It's a bit of solitude. I find it really quite therapeutic."

Arlene Dickinson, one of the business titans on CBC's *Dragon's Den*, says she took up running to lose weight but discovered one day that she was hooked.

"The first time I ran 15k I thought, 'Wow, that felt amazing!'" she said. "I ran for that long and I felt so good afterwards. Maybe I had been loving it for a while, but that time I noticed and thought, 'This is great.' It wasn't that I didn't love it up until then, I just hadn't stopped and realized that I was loving it so much."

For Ottawa Senators captain Daniel Alfredsson, running is another outlet for his competitive streak. "Even though I'm a little bit better about it, I still need a time," he said. "It's a competitive thing. There have been a few times where I go out and just take it easy, but somehow I've always got to try to beat the time before. I have a tough time just going out running. I've gotta go fast."

Like many other runners, two CBC personalities share a fear of injury causing an interruption in their training. Dickinson says she dreads getting injured. Solomon hurt his knee playing hockey and his first reaction was, "Will I be able to run?" He said, "All I'm thinking is: I'm screwed for running. It's a big part of my life."

Just like us.

[THE ELUSIVE RUNNER'S HIGH]

iRun for the natural high ODESSA BEZANSON, NOVA SCOTIA

Anyone who doubts the existence of the runner's high has never been in Canada on the first weekend of spring weather. Feelings of euphoria and jubilation? All it takes is to be able to run in a pair of shorts after a gruelling and prolonged winter.

Leaving aside the joy of running unencumbered by heavy clothing, the runner's high has always something more connected to lore than science. But it's been a longstanding source of debate for everyone from sprinters to neurosurgeons. The runner's high is as elusive a notion as the all-powerful deity: Some people swear it exists, others are non-believers and in between are a few who have had only a fleeting relationship with it.

Some runners claim they experience a runner's high on a regular basis. At the other end of the spectrum are those for whom running is like hitting your head against a wall: the only pleasure comes when you stop.

As the non-believers might point out, feeling good after a hard workout shouldn't be surprising. Just because you get a sense of achievement or general well-being doesn't prove anything magical is at play.

And even if the finish line of a race may make you very emotional – I've come close to sobbing at the end of marathons – you might just be happy about an accomplishment. That doesn't mean you're experiencing a runner's high. Otherwise there would be a math-quiz high as well.

The runner's high is supposed to be something more than that. The sensations are supposed to be comparable to those produced by a mood-altering drug. Yet for more than thirty years, the concept of the runner's high was considered unproven, at least scientifically. For decades, researchers were never able to replicate the event in a laboratory. A couple of studies even proved it didn't exist. Maybe that's because it's hard to feel "high" when there are all kinds of wires attached to you.

But in 2008, researchers in Germany announced in the journal *Cerebral Cortex* (free map of the hippocampus with every subscription!) that the runner's high really exists and that endorphins are responsible.

The researchers studied brain scans of runners before and after long workouts and used new chemicals that are able to demonstrate the presence of endorphins. The study wasn't large – only ten distance runners were scanned. But the data showed that endorphins were produced during a run and they were attaching themselves to the parts of the brain that are associated with emotions. And standard psychological testing showed the moods of the runners after their long run matched the amount of endorphins present in their brains. More endorphins, more euphoria.

Several independent researchers quickly accepted the findings, including one who was quoted in the *New York Times* as saying, "This is the first time someone took this head on." (Get it? Those neuroscientists!)

But more recent research suggests that while they may be

more prevalent after a good workout, endorphin molecules are too big to make it into the brain's pleasure centre. Instead, it's the presence of endocannabinoids in the bloodstream that is responsible for the high associated with exercise.

Researchers have done all kinds of tests on rats and mice and they've concluded that the body has a bunch of receptors that, when connected with these endocannabinoids, reduce feelings of pain and increase a sense of well-being. The endocannabinoids, which are a substance similar to that found in marijuana, help push us towards exercise and promote our enjoyment of a good workout.

Does that create the runner's high? The rats and mice were unable to answer detailed questions about their emotions while on their tiny treadmills. But it's the closest explanation to date.

Regardless of the science, the nearest I've come to experiencing it was during a particularly fast 10k run on a cool night. I was running as hard as I could, but I seemed to move past the usual pain and anguish of a tough run into feeling like I could go on forever. My feet felt like they were barely touching the ground.

I'm not sure if it was a runner's high, or if it was caused by endorphins or endocannabiwhatsits, but it felt pretty good.

$$\left[\ \textbf{ONE DAY OUT OF FIFTY}\ \right]$$

iRun to prove to myself that I can accomplish anything NAOMI OSBORNE, NEW BRUNSWICK

Dean Karnazes is lying on his back on Heartbreak Hill. He has been running a marathon every day for almost a month and now, midway through the legendary climb thirty-two kilometres into the Boston Marathon course, Karnazes is down on the pavement. Runners are passing him on both sides. "I can't take Heartbreak Hill," he shouts. Still, on the slope that is said to have claimed the dreams of hundreds of runners, Karnazes is not in any pain at all. He is only hamming it up for a laugh. A second later, he springs to his feet and sprints ahead to catch up with the group that passed.

Heartbreak Hill is no test at all for Karnazes. Nor is running twenty-nine marathons in twenty-nine days.

This is a guy who once ran 560 kilometres continuously, going three nights without sleep, and has won the Badwater Ultramarathon, a 216-kilometre race across Death Valley in the middle of the summer.

His current test was spread out over seven weeks plus a day. Starting September 17, 2006 in Missouri, he had run a marathon every day in a different state. His goal was to complete fifty marathons in fifty consecutive days in all fifty states, finishing November 5 in New York.

Imagine planning a trip in which you would visit all fifty U.S. states in just fifty days. Think how exhausting the travel would be. Now picture running a marathon each time you get there.

I had to train for weeks and then rest for a few days just to be able to run one marathon with Karnazes. In each stop along his journey, Karnazes ran with up to fifty people who signed up through his website. I chose Boston because it was a chance to run the legendary course for the first time. (I was still a long way from meeting the qualifying time to enter the actual race.)

I arrived in Hopkinton, Massachusetts, a quaint colonial town of 14,000 people that is, by virtue of it being exactly 42.2 kilometres from downtown Boston, home to the start line for the Boston Marathon course.

After a quick introduction from Karnazes, we were off. It was a crisp and clear autumn day, perfect running weather, and the fall colours made for a spectacular route. I did my best to balance two goals: running a marathon and trying to learn as much about Karnazes as possible.

I wasn't sure what to expect of him. In pictures, he has his game face on, a hardened look of determination and focus that rivals Lance Armstrong's.

In person, though, Karnazes was enthusiastic and social. Perhaps, after running in solitude so often, he was glad for the company. He acted as host and leader, offering water and food to his fellow runners, trying to learn as much about them as he could. A few kilometres after we first met, he caught up to me again. "How's my man from Canada?" he said.

I asked him why he was running fifty marathons in fifty days and, after joking "I don't have a car," he said he wanted to do something inclusive. He was concerned about the rising rate of obesity in the United States and wanted to draw attention to physical fitness. The money raised from this event went to his foundation, which promotes physical activity for children.

The travel was gruelling, he said, but he was enjoying the people he met along the way. He pointed out a woman who had joined him for three other marathons in the past month and was, today in Boston, running her 100th marathon. He also said he was told there was someone in our group who was running for the very first time in his life.

"That's crazy," Karnazes said.

"No, what you're doing is crazy," said one of the other runners.

His favourite story is about a runner from Japan who joined him last month in Hawaii. The man was on his honeymoon and was running with Karnazes to prove he was worthy of his new wife. Karnazes asked him if he was tired from his wedding night, "Oh no," the man said. "I saved myself for the marathon."

At the halfway point of the race, we were joined by a group of runners from the cross-country running team from Wellesley College, a university for women. One of the new runners asked, "Which one of you is Dean?" and about four of us replied, "I am."

Thanks to the new runners with fresh legs, the pace picked up in the second half and a group of about twenty of us crossed the finish line with Dean in a little less than four hours.

A few minutes later, I glanced at Dean and noticed he didn't seem to have broken a sweat. That's impressive.

But not as much as the fact that, while I was resting from our run together the next day, he ran another marathon.

[**ROUND AND ROUND THE GRAVESTONES**]

iRun because I want to live to be 100 COLETTE DEJEAN, ONTARIO

I was already impressed with Ed Whitlock before I met him in 2008. Then I found out about his training regimen.

Whitlock doesn't just defy aging with his world-record, age-group race performances, such as becoming the first person over seventy to run a marathon in less than three hours. He defies logic with his relentless routine.

To train for a marathon, Whitlock runs for three hours a day, seven days a week. And if you're searching for a metaphor for a man who has cheated aging, he does all his running in a cemetery. Round and round the gravestones he runs, as if he's taunting the gods who have pried younger men from their lives while he's maintained impossible racing times.

The loop is only a third of a mile, so he can end up running it sixty times or more. He doesn't bring any water and doesn't count his laps or measure how far he's run. He carries only a watch so he knows when it's time to stop.

"Absolutely, it gets boring," he says. "But for me, it has some advantages. It's just 200 yards from home. In the winter, you don't run against the wind for any length of time, and they clear the road. In the summer, most of it's in the shade.

"I never claim that's what everybody ought to do, but it works for me."

Whitlock was always a fast runner. He was a competitive athlete in high school in England. He gave up running when he moved to Canada, but took it up again in his forties, racing internationally in middle-distance events. He won the World Masters in the 1500 metres for men forty-five and older in 1979.

That year, he also ran a 2:31 marathon, which he now says "wasn't bad for a middle-distance runner."

"I was forty-eight, so I was getting old," says Whitlock.

His running dwindled again in his fifties, but he took up long-distance running in his sixties and started knocking down one record after another.

He ran a series of sub-three-hour marathons in his late-sixties and got the idea that he might be able to do it in his seventies.

"That was an objective worth going for," he says.

In 2001, at the age of seventy, he came up just short. At a marathon in London, Ontario, he finished in 3:00:24. It was a world record for anyone over seventy, but it wasn't fast enough.

After taking a year off because of an injury, he trained for the Scotiabank Toronto Waterfront Marathon in 2003 and planned to try again to break three hours. But six days before the marathon, he was almost knocked out of the race.

"I was walking over to the mall and I was walking along quite briskly and I managed to do a face plant on the sidewalk," he says. "I found out afterwards that I broke my nose. I had two black eyes and all kinds of abrasions all over my face. It wasn't a pretty sight."

Whitlock says many people told him not to run the race, but he did it anyway. He was ahead of his goal pace at 35k, but then it started getting tougher.

"It was a real struggle to get home," he says. "Fortunately I got in with a little group of runners that helped me along. I stayed with this group, grimly hanging on, until about forty or forty-one. And one guy stayed with me and shepherded me home."

He finished in a time of 2:59:08, becoming the oldest person ever to break three hours.

"The photographs of me finishing are not pretty. I had all these facial disfigurements for one thing, and I was showing obvious distress apart from that. I was leaning over to one side. I was happy to have got it done, but I was still embarrassed about the way I finished and the way I looked. It was a feeling more of relief than elation."

The next year was a different story. At seventy-three years old, he ran the Toronto Waterfront again and finished in 2:54:48.

"It was an absolutely marvellous race," he says. "I wish I knew how you could do that all the time. It would be nice to be able to bottle it. I finished in great shape, I wasn't in any distress."

How is Whitlock able to do it? Not even he is sure.

"I suppose a large part is genetics," he says. "I suspect that's more than ninety per cent of it. I'm naturally light, I have good mechanics. I don't pound as much as most people would do."

And although he's occasionally sidelined by an injury, he has no intention of stopping.

"Do I have any thoughts that I'll be running in my nineties? Yeah. I'll run as long as I can.

"I'd just like to keep running, mainly. That's what I'd like to do. And set some eighty-year-old records, maybe. They're well within reach if I could keep running."

[BLOOD, SWEAT AND OTHER FLUIDS]

iRun for the after-effects COLLEEN HUDSON, QUEBEC

It seems simple enough. You buy a pair of running shoes, you tie up the laces, and then you start putting one foot in front of the other.

And certainly running is a lot less complicated and high-maintenance than most other sports, like auto racing. I'm proud to say I know how to change a tire on my bicycle, but that's about the extent of my mechanical capacity. At least a runner doesn't need a tool kit or a selection of spare parts. Toss out one pair of shoes and get another. Maybe tighten a screw on your sunglasses. That's it.

But running is not without its technical knowledge. Just as cyclists get to know their bikes, runners become acutely aware of their most important piece of equipment: their bodies. And that goes well beyond the science of kinetics, the data about anaerobic threshold and lactic acid and VO2 max.

For the new runner, there is a series of surprising little discoveries, the delicate intricacies of the sport and its impact on the body that you might never have pictured. To the non-runner, these are the unknown unknowns.

Cyclists compare crank sets and carbon wheels. Runners talk about blisters and loose toenails.

I've taken off a shoe after a long run to see a large blood stain on my sock, the result of a sharp toenail rubbing against an adjacent toe repeatedly over twenty kilometres.

After my first marathon, I was afraid to remove my socks. Based on the pain, I was expecting to see a big blistery mess of damaged toes and toenails.

It turns out I had one purple toenail on my right foot and it wasn't as bad as I first thought. A new toenail grew in under it over the next two months and then the dead one fell off. Still, I thought of it as a bit of a badge of honour. I'm not into tattoos, but what's the point of running that far without having some reminder of your accomplishment on your body, at least for a while?

Of course, it isn't just your feet that become susceptible to the ravages of friction and repeated motion. At one marathon, I remember volunteers handing out tongue dispensers with little slabs of vaseline on them. The aid station was placed strategically at about twenty-five kilometres into the race, when a little lubricant sometimes comes in handy.

"What the heck is that for?" one runner called out as he passed by the station. Ah, that's for a little word that's seldom used in polite company outside of the running sphere: chafing. I've never applied vaseline during a race (or any other activity, for that matter) but I've tried several different pairs of shorts in a race to see which were the most friendly to my nether regions. In the end I found a pair of triathlon shorts served me best.

No discussion about the delicate aspects of running would be complete without touching on – if you'll excuse that expression – bloody nipples. I remember the first time I got home from a run of over twenty-five kilometres on a hot day. When the water from the shower hit my chest I thought I was being subjected to a special kind of torture.

No one had warned me about this. Until the end of my shower, I searched my mind for every possible explanation for this sudden pain in an unusual location and couldn't come up with anything. I checked my shirt when I got out and found little red smudges. Fortunately a quick Google search convinced me it was a fairly common occurrence and I wasn't suffering from some bizarre and embarrassing new ailment.

Since then, I've had a series of marathon photos ruined by red patches on my chest and I've taken to wearing darker material on race day. When my wife asked iRun's creative director for a photo for my fortieth birthday party, Lisa replied with a photo from the Mississauga Marathon and a quick question: "Bloody nipples: yes/no?"

Blood isn't the only bodily fluid that becomes part of a runner's repertoire. I actually considered calling this book *There Will Be Sweat*. No matter what time of year, no matter how sophisticated the clothing, I seem to have a tremendous capacity to perspire that continues even after a post-run shower.

And finally, on winter runs, there is the delicate matter of the runny nose. It's not unusual to find yourself, in the absence of tissue, putting a finger to one nostril and clearing out the other one. Unfortunately, my friend Bob once thought I was running on his left when I was actually on his right and I ended up running through a cloud of his mucus. It's not difficult for me to call up an image of that moment, so firmly is it imprinted in my memory.

But after a while, a running partner is like a spouse, someone who has the privilege of not only hearing about your chafing and blisters, but actually enduring all of your various bodily sounds. Over a series of long runs, you become immune to what might be considered gross at a cocktail party or workplace. So, what's a little mucus between friends?

[THE OVER-CONFIDENT NOVICE]

iRun hard. If it was easy, everyone would do it NICOLE MICKELOW, ONTARIO

Okay, I couldn't help myself. Maybe I was being a bit of a running snob. But is it so wrong to take some satisfaction from working hard to stay in shape when you get the chance to prove it against someone who's not, but thinks he is?

I encourage as many people as I can to take up running, although taking up this good habit is a bit like trying to get someone to stop a bad one: They have to want to do it. You can only offer your support.

So without being pushy, I'm a bit of a running evangelist. And the last thing I would want to do is discourage a budding runner.

But I couldn't help feeling a small twinge of guilty pleasure when I taught a little bit of a lesson to a young guy who thought running would be easy.

Pat (not his real name) was a likeable work colleague, about fifteen years younger than me. He flirted with taking up running a few times, but never got serious about it. But he liked to tease his girlfriend, who was a runner, that he would quickly train for a 10k and finish ahead of her. So he was due for a little karma or comeuppance.

When I stayed at their home on a quick visit to Toronto, I mentioned I was going to go for a run.

"Great, maybe we can run together," Pat said.

"Have you been doing much running?" I asked.

"A little bit."

"Are you sure you want to do this?" his girlfriend joined in.

"No problem," said Pat.

After I changed into my running gear, I went looking for Pat. He wasn't in the kitchen or the living room. I checked the rest of the house. Not there either. I poked my head outside. There he stood, in his shorts, T-shirt and running shoes, in the open doorway of his garage.

Smoking a cigarette.

"That's a good place to start," I said.

Pat said he would be ready after he finished his butt and chugged down a bottle of Gatorade. He seemed to think the Gatorade would offset the smoking.

We set off on a five-kilometre loop his girlfriend had mapped out for her runs. I didn't run at my fastest possible pace, but I have to admit I pushed a little harder than on a normal easy run. I wanted to see how long Pat could hang on.

We maintained a bit of a conversation over the first few hundred metres. Then the gaps started getting longer. After a few minutes, Pat asked how far we had run.

"Nine hundred metres," I said.

"How many kilometres is that?" Pat asked. Something was already happening to his brain.

We ran another 500 metres and crossed an intersection without stopping.

"I was praying for that light to change," said Pat.

A few minutes later, he said he might turn back at 2.5k so that he ran a total of 5k.

"But this is a 5k loop," I said, not wanting to let him off the hook. "You don't need to turn around." We kept going.

At about 2k, we stopped at a red light. Pat put his hands on his knees.

I was beginning to worry if I was inflicting some type of damage on Pat. Maybe I should give him a way out of the rest of the run. Then he caught his breath and said, "I think I'm going to walk for a bit. I'll start running again after I've had a bit of a break."

I carried on. I looked over my shoulder a few times and saw Pat was still walking. At about 3.5k, I decided that rather than doing a 5k loop, I'd turn around and run back the way I came. That would give me a total run of seven kilometres. It would also give me a chance to check on Pat.

I ran back about a kilometre and reached the bottom of the hill. Pat was at the top, still walking. When he saw me, he started running again.

I stopped when I reached him.

"I guess I'm not in as good shape as I thought I was," he said.

Most people don't think running is easy. In fact, most non-runners probably think it's harder than it really is. But there are a few people like Pat who think there's nothing to it. And even though I know I shouldn't, I still can't help feeling a little bit satisfied at proving him wrong.

[THE PRODIGY RETURNS]

iRun because I love to go fast KATHLEEN WILKER, ONTARIO

In 1967, Canada was celebrating its 100th birthday and the sport of women's distance running was in its infancy. And on May 6 of that year, somewhere in between a historic first for a female runner and a nation's centennial party, a thirteen-year-old Canadian girl set the world record for the women's marathon.

The 1960s were a decade of hope and optimism, but it was also a time when long-distance races still were not supposed to be run by women, let alone children who were barely in their teenage years.

Only weeks earlier, Kathrine Switzer had entered the Boston Marathon, from which women were banned, using only her initials on the registration form. When one race official saw her on the course, he practically assaulted her. After her boyfriend fought off the attack, Switzer finished the race, becoming the first registered woman ever to run Boston. As her reward, within days she was expelled from the athletic federation in the United States.

Meanwhile, in Canada, another story was unfolding. Sy Mah, a teacher and running coach who would go on to incredible marathon achievements of his own, was coaching a young girl to pursue a world record.

Maureen Wilton started running when she was nine. Now

Maureen Mancuso, she remembers the day when her older brother came home with a ribbon from a track meet and she and another brother decided they each wanted one too. Her parents enrolled them in the North York Track Club, which Mah had founded at the school where he was teaching.

"My brother quit after about a year," says Mancuso, "but I kept going."

The club was considered one of the best in North America and young Maureen was one of its top athletes. In the spring of 1967, Mah approached her about running a marathon.

"I don't even think I knew how far a marathon was," says Mancuso. "I think I asked him how far and then I said yes. He asked me if I wanted to go for the record. I said sure."

Mah trained Wilton for a marathon in May at York University. And after reading about Switzer, he invited her to Toronto to run in the same race. Since it was just sixteen days after Boston, Switzer didn't expect to turn in a great performance.

But she was glad to get the call.

"We were persona non grata in the United States," says Switzer. "So it was a big deal that we were invited and welcome. It was the beginning of a wonderful love affair that I had with Canada. It was a very open and enthusiastic place."

After finishing a class on a Friday at Syracuse University, Switzer and her friends piled into a car and drove up to Toronto, stopping at Niagara Falls on the way. She ran and walked the race at a slow pace, still hobbling from Boston. Somewhere ahead of her that day was Wilton.

The course was five loops and Wilton ran the first three with her coach. Runners from her track club ran the last two loops with her. Mah went on to finish the race, his first marathon. He ran

523 more over the next twenty years, which was the most by any runner in the world when he died in 1988.

At various points on each lap, Wilton got updates from supporters who told her where she stood against the record pace.

"All of a sudden, with one mile to go, my mother said, 'Oh, my watch was wrong, you're never going to make it,'" Mancuso remembers. "I said, 'What? I've just run twenty-five miles and you're telling me I'm not going to make it?'"

She ran the last mile in six minutes, much faster than any other, and finished in a record time of 3:15:23.

"She thought her watch was wrong but it wasn't," says Mancuso. "I can laugh now."

Wilton's first marathon was the fastest ever by a female runner. The news was reported around the world, but Switzer says when she met the new record holder after the race, it didn't seem to have made a big impression on the teenager.

"She was thirteen but she was very much a little girl," says Switzer. "She was just a little stick. I remember her being such a lean little kid with short dark hair and great big eyes. I walked up to her after the race and I said, 'Wow, that was incredible what you did today.'

"She said, 'I'm really not crazy about running. What I really like are The Monkees.'"

Mancuso says she ran in a few more events, but lost interest in running as her friends started dropping out of the track club.

By the time she was seventeen, she wasn't running at all.

She eventually married, had two children and launched a career in the financial industry. More recently, she found a new passion – working part-time in a pet store. Along the way, she has occasionally entered a neighbourhood fun run, but it wasn't until her daughter started running that she took up the sport again.

"My daughter came home in Grade 2 and said she wanted to join the track club," she says. "I said, 'What do you want to do that for?'"

Carolyn Mancuso proved to be just like her mom. She eventually earned a track scholarship at a U.S. college.

When Maureen Mancuso started running again as an adult, she found a love of the sport that exceeded what she felt as a teenager. She joined a running club in Toronto and has participated in a few smaller events.

And in October 2009, she ran the half-marathon at the GoodLife Fitness Toronto Marathon, and Switzer joined her.

Even though they hadn't spoken for forty years, the two were always linked by the events of 1967. Mancuso says she's proud not just of her record, which was broken three months later by a West German runner, but the fact that she was a pioneer in women's distance running.

"I look back on that and I'm glad I was a part of changing history," she says. "We were changing the course of the sport for women. Women weren't allowed to run. They didn't think we were capable of it."

[**THE UNLIKELY ATHLETES**]

iRun because this addiction is better than my last LARRY BRADLEY, ONTARIO

In a marathon, all runners follow the same route to the finish line. But the road to the starting line is different for everyone.

There are stories of overcoming loss, of fighting illness, of losing weight. There are amusing tales and heartbreaking narratives. There are natural athletes and unlikely ones. But you'd have a difficult time finding any roads to the marathon as improbable, compelling, shocking and inspiring as these.

In 2008, eight men each ran their first marathon. They were among the most unlikely of athletes. All eight were recovering drug addicts from Harvest House, a residential treatment program in Ottawa. You think you've come a long way in your training? Look at the life these guys were leading not too long ago.

"I started using drugs at the age of twelve," says David Gagnon. "I was always skipping school, dropping out. I wasn't able to graduate Grade 10. The last two months before I went into Harvest House, I was using cocaine heavily."

"I've been an addict since I was seventeen," says Peter Bédard. After a series of thefts, break-and-enters and armed robberies, Bédard says he served a two-year sentence that finished in 2006. "Not even seven days later, I committed another robbery."

"I was a mixed-up kid," says James Reynolds. "I got in with the wrong crowd, started doing residential crime and was arrested three times."

"I used crack cocaine every day for a four-year stretch," says Trevor Struth, "to dull the pain that marijuana and alcohol couldn't."

A few years ago, the Harvest House runners were all on a path to self-destruction, getting high on hard drugs. Then the eight of them – Gagnon, Bédard, Reynolds, Struth, Eric Ruhl, Tom Mekarski, Brent McRann and John Hambleton –discovered a new buzz: the runner's high.

"It's a good high," says Gagnon. "When I'm running, I get a buzz from life."

"This lifestyle is way better by far," says Bédard. "I wouldn't trade it for anything."

The group was trained by Ottawa coach and Running Room regional manager Phil Marsh, and was led by Gary Wand, a program director at Harvest House, who started the running program the previous year. Both Marsh and Wand trained with the eight runners each week and joined them in the Ottawa Marathon.

From the time the program started until race day, not one runner dropped out. It's as if all that energy that used to be consumed by destructive behaviour has now been channelled into running.

"It's kind of like drugs," says Gagnon. "I always want to do more, to go higher. When I get into something, like drugs, I get into it deeply."

Gagnon and several of the other runners are convinced that running will help them stick to the right path.

"I know that if I use again, I won't be able to run," says Gagnon, who also quit smoking in the year before his first marathon. "It's one or the other."

"This is the best experience of my life," says Struth. "It's easier to get drunk or stoned and not face life. But I want to quit every time I run."

"The thing that keeps me sober," says Reynolds, "is that I can work out and feel good after."

Reynolds went on to take a civil engineering course at university. "To go from being a homeless guy breaking into people's houses to going to university," he says, "is a miracle."

For Bédard, who ended up working at Harvest House, it was an opportunity to prove something not just to himself, but to the men who followed him into the program.

"I'm showing to the addicts that they have a chance," says Bédard. "They have a choice. If someone who screwed up his life the way I did can make it, they can make it."

"Running saved my life," says Struth. "I'm not a guy that faces challenges. I run away. But we're starting something and we're finishing it. This is the first taste of me saying something and really doing it.

"This is the hardest thing I've ever done," he says. "But I know if I can run a marathon, I can do anything."

That's the way a lot of runners feel. But it may not seem as improbable for them to be saying it, or mean as much to be doing it, as it does for Struth and the other seven athletes from Harvest House.

[37,000 STORIES]

iRun because it inspires me to inspire others JENNA LADD, ONTARIO

There was a man running the New York City Marathon with me in November 2006 who started running nineteen years earlier in a prison yard in South Africa under apartheid. He ran around a tiny square, one hundred paces on each side, for up to an hour. This was to be his first marathon.

There was a woman running her first marathon that day who quit smoking on Christmas Day the previous year. "When I am running, all my cares slip away," she wrote on the New York marathon's website. "I feel whole, healthy, and healed. The sport unlocked something inside me that makes me so proud of myself."

There's a woman who was running that day to raise money for autism, which afflicts both her sons.

There were thousands of others who were running to raise money for causes just as close to their hearts.

There were moms and dads and grandparents.

There were people running for their moms and dads and grandparents.

There were people who had survived cancer.

There were people who had survived cancer more than once.

There was a disabled Israeli veteran who was once almost given up for dead, who would be handcycling her way through the course.

There was a NewYork police officer who suffered a bullet wound that paralysed his left leg from the knee down, and voluntarily had it amputated so he could maintain an active lifestyle, including marathon running, on a prosthetic leg.

There were more than 150 people in wheelchairs.

There was a forty-three-year-old New York priest who was attacked by a gang of teenagers eighteen months earlier and was in intensive care for nine days. He wanted to finish in 2:45.

There were people who finally got off the couch and started exercising and this is what it led to.

There was a visually impaired runner who was trying to set a world record.

There was at least one Radio City Rockette, at least one fortysomething former supermodel, at least one Broadway actor from Monty Python's Spamalot, and at least one network television news correspondent.

There was the governor of Arkansas, a future presidential candidate who three years earlier weighed 300 pounds and was diagnosed with type II diabetes.

There was Paul Tergat, then the world-record holder in the marathon and the 2005 New York champion, who was back to defend his title.

There was Hendrick Ramaala, the 2004 winner who battled Tergat in a remarkable sprint to the finish the previous year and lost by three-tenths of a second. "That pain has motivated me to come back and run in New York again," he wrote on the marathon's website.

There was a woman who was a spectator during the emotional

New York Marathon of 2001, just weeks after September 11, and vowed to run it herself one day. "It is not a big thing in life's grand scheme, especially when you consider the five-year anniversary we are commemorating this fall," she wrote. "But with every step, we, the runners of the ING New York City Marathon 2006, will embrace and celebrate the beauty and splendour that is this resilient city, this remarkable state, and this most amazing of countries."

There was Lance Armstrong, the seven-time Tour de France winner who was called the world's fittest first-time marathon runner. He said he was hoping to finish in 2:45 to 3:00, but a lot of people thought he could go faster than that.

And there was me.

My story wasn't very compelling and my finishing time wasn't going to be very impressive, but I was thrilled to be running one of the world's great marathons in one of the world's great cities. I was excited about seeing autumn in New York, on foot, about running through the five boroughs, in sight of the Statue of Liberty and Yankee Stadium. I was fired up about running past two million cheering New Yorkers on a course that's like the world's longest parade route. I liked the idea that I was running with Lance Armstrong, even though my best shot at seeing him was going to be on the evening news.

But most of all, I was inspired by the stirring examples of all the other runners. In some pictures they would seem like tiny dots in a mosaic, but each had a separate narrative starting a few months or a lifetime earlier and finishing that day in the New York City Marathon, the race with 37,000 stories.

[IF YOU CAN MAKE IT THERE]

iRun to be the best version of myself that I can be JACKIE DESCHENES, ONTARIO

Time for which my alarm clock was set to wake me up for the New York City Marathon on November 5, 2006: 3:55 a.m.

Time I woke up: 3:50 a.m.

Number of New York street vendors who wished me luck in the marathon between 4:30 and 5 a.m.: 3

Minutes it took for the shuttle bus to drive from midtown Manhattan to Staten Island, where the race started: 40

Amount of time, in minutes, I spent thinking about the fact that it took 40 minutes to drive from near the finish line to the starting line and that I was going to run all the way back: 4

Number of volunteers who clapped and cheered as we disembarked from the bus: 30

Time I arrived at the staging area: 5:35 a.m.

Scheduled start time of the New York City Marathon: 10:10 a.m.

Temperature in degrees Celsius in New York at 5:35 a.m.: 5

Number of people I could see shivering in the staging area: 5

Number of people who joined me in crowding around the warm exhaust air from an electric generator: 7

Number of holes burned into my running pants when my leg got too close to the generator: 1

Number of different countries represented by the eight people

I chatted with in the staging area: 7

Number of people who were from the small town in England where my father grew up: 1

Number of minutes before the race when I began wondering why I ever decided to run marathons: 5

Number of minutes into the race before I remembered why I decided to run marathons: 1

Number of helicopters circling above the start line: 9

Number of items of clothing I discarded either just before or just after the start and will never see again: 2

Number of minutes it took me to run to the start line after the gun went off: 5

Number of lines of *New York, New York*, the first song played after the gun, that I and the other runners near me were able to hear and sing along with before the song was over: 2

Number of minutes into the race I stopped feeling cold and started feeling warm: 4

Number of runners I saw peeing off the side of the upper level of the Verrazano Narrows Bridge: 15

Number of runners I spoke to after the race who were running on the lower level of the bridge and made a point of staying as far away from the side as possible: 1

Number of children who gave me high-fives in the first five kilometres of the race: 12

Number who were wearing plastic gloves for hygienic purposes: 3

Number of other runners I encountered with the name "Mark" on their shirts, prompting spectators to shout, "Go, Mark!": 12

Number of people with "Jimbo" on their shirts, prompting shouts of "Go, Jimbo!": 1

Number of spectators' signs and exhortations to cheer by

course-side bandleaders that contained profanity: 2

Number of fans on the Queensboro Bridge from Queens into Manhattan: 0

Estimated number of fans greeting runners at the end of the bridge on 1st Avenue: 5,000

Estimated number of beats per minute increase in my heart rate on hearing the roar of the crowd: 10

Number of sports gels I consumed during the first 19 miles of the marathon: 4

Number of minutes I spent in a porta-potty at Mile 19 because the gels didn't agree with me: 6

Number of gels consumed in the rest of the marathon: 0

Number of different flavours of Gatorade available at the 23 aid stations on the course: 1

Number of cups of lemon-lime Gatorade I consumed during the marathon: 14

Estimated number of months before I will be able to consume a cup of lemon-lime Gatorade again: 24

Combined total number of glimpses I had of the Statue of Liberty, Yankee Stadium, Lance Armstrong or anyone from Kenya: 0

Ranking of running a marathon among the hardest things Lance Armstrong has ever done, according to Armstrong during a post-race news conference: 1

Minimum number of rows of people lining the final seven kilometres of the race: 5

Number of times in the final three kilometres that spectators shouted something so encouraging that, in my weakened state, I almost teared up: 3

My unofficial finishing time, not adjusted for my bathroom

break: four hours two minutes.

Number of minutes after the race I stopped feeling warm and starting feeling cold: 5

Number of minutes it took me to walk from the finish line to the very first truck that carried checked bags for the marathon runners: 25

Number of the truck holding my checked bag: 64

Total number of minutes it took me to walk to the exit and family reunion area for people with surnames beginning with the letter S: 54

Number of contestants from The Amazing Race I met in the family reunion area: 4

Estimated number of New Yorkers who congratulated me during my trip from the finish line to my hotel room: 25

Places in the world I would rather have been than running the New York City Marathon that day: 0

[A LEG TO RUN ON]

*iRun to test my limits and show people what is possible
if you put your mind to it* RICK BALL, ONTARIO

When you break the world record in the marathon and the 10k in the same year, what do you do next?

If you're Rick Ball, the answer is: you go for the record in the half-marathon.

Having set world records for single-leg amputees at the Boston Marathon and Ottawa Race Weekend in 2009, Ball set his eyes on the Army Race half-marathon that September in Ottawa. Not bad for a guy who wasn't even running two years earlier.

At the age of forty-three, Ball suddenly became a budding running star who was training for a chance to represent Canada at the 2012 Paralympic Games in London. He quickly won the attention of Athletics Canada, the sport's governing body, which invited him to race against able-bodied athletes at the Canadian Track and Field Championships in Toronto and then join their training camp in Windsor.

"Two years and look how far I've come," says Ball, a Toronto subway mechanic who lives in Orillia.

He is as surprised as anyone at his world-class status. He wasn't even a runner when, in 1986 at twenty-one, he lost his leg in a motorcycle crash.

"I thought my life was over," he says. "I was devastated. My goal at the time was to cover it up, not let anyone know. I'd always wear pants. I went from that to the complete opposite now."

After recovering, Ball started participating in sports such as cycling and cross-country skiing. He wanted to try running, but could never find a prosthetic leg that wouldn't reopen his scars.

Then he was introduced by a prosthetics expert to a powerful carbon-fibre leg on which he could run without pain. The problem was the leg cost almost $10,000.

"I said to him, 'Forget it, that's too much money.' But he was a good salesman. He said, give it a try, we can always send it back.

"Once I tried it out, there was no going back. Now it's my most prized possession besides my family. It makes me whole again."

With a powerful new leg and a new lease on life, Ball set some ambitious targets.

"I had this goal in mind that I wanted to do the Boston Marathon," he says. "I spent all that money on the leg. I figured if I'm going to do this, let's do it right."

He contacted Roger DePlancke, a veteran marathon runner and coach. When DePlancke heard how little experience Ball had, he almost laughed.

DePlancke figured it would take a few races for Ball to qualify for Boston, but in 2008 in Mississauga, in his first attempt, Ball finished in 3:17:38. As an athlete with a disability, he could have qualified with a much slower finish, but his performance was faster than even the Boston qualifying time for an able-bodied athlete his age.

Ball set his sights on a new challenge: a world record. He found out that the fastest marathon for a single-leg amputee was 3:04 and set out to break it in Boston. He struggled over the final two kilometres, and was so dehydrated he needed treatment. But he finished in 3:01:50.

A few weeks after Boston, veteran elite marathoner Tania Jones e-mailed Ball to suggest he go for another record in Ottawa. With the crowd cheering him loudly, Ball broke the 10k record by four seconds.

Then in September, Ball completed his hat-trick by setting the half-marathon record at the Army Run. He's since become the first single-leg amputee to break three hours in the marathon.

When he competed against Canada's best able-bodied 10k runners at the national track and field championships, he came within half a minute of his Ottawa time, but ran the final two laps alone after all the able-bodied athletes had finished. Nevertheless, officials presented him with a gold medal.

That experience, he hopes, was a little bit of foreshadowing to 2012. "To be in London in 2012 and represent Canada, that's my next big huge goal."

But world records or not, he's just happy to be a runner.

"I'm just doing something I like," he says. "All this other stuff is kind of a bonus.

"Someone said to me, 'Can you imagine how fast you would run if you had your real leg?' And I said, I probably wouldn't even be running."

$$\left[\text{ IT PROBABLY WON'T KILL YOU } \right]$$

iRun to enjoy life, stay healthy and live longer IAN YOUNG, ONTARIO

When an unusual event happens three times in the same day, it's hard not to suspect a trend. So it's not surprising the deaths of three runners in a half-marathon in Detroit provoked a series of articles and blog postings about the risks of long-distance running. One headline, in a weekly newspaper in Tennessee, referred to the marathon as a "killer event."

But even though it has some risk, long-distance running remains a very safe sport. Of course it's worrisome to hear about people dying while participating in an activity you do four or five times a week. And there were alarming circumstances about the deaths in the half-marathon in 2009, including that all three runners were described by family members as being in excellent health and having trained for the race, and that two of them were under forty.

So, understanding the risks and the realities of long-distance running is important. There are some key points to remember.

For one, the odds of death are very low. Dr. William Roberts, the medical director of the Twin Cities Marathon in Minnesota, told Health magazine, "More people die from lightning strikes while golfing. And it's probably safer to be running in these races than driving a car."

That last point may be true. University of Toronto researchers published a study in the British Medical Journal that put the odds of a runner dying in a marathon at less than one in 100,000. The odds of a person dying by driving the same forty-two-kilometre route in a car were twice as high.

It might be as simple as this: More people are dying because more people are running. The running boom means that many race events, like Detroit, have 20,000 participants or more. And the increase to the running population has come in part from runners who are older and in part from those who are less fit, so some doctors feel the odds of a cardiac event have increased. But even something that happens to one in 100,000 will occur much more often in an annual event with 20,000 participants than in one with 500.

Also, randomness plays a role. It was surprising that three deaths occurred in the same event, especially since the weather was cool and there was nothing especially challenging or different about the course. But Leonard Mlodinow, the author of the bestseller The Drunkard's Walk: How Randomness Rules Our Lives, would point out that rare events are not always evenly distributed. Something with a one-in-100,000 chance of happening can happen three times on the same day and then not again for ten years. In fact, before this year, the Detroit marathon hadn't experienced a fatality in fifteen years.

Pre-existing conditions are usually a factor. Autopsy results might shed more light on the exact causes of an individual death while running, but many people who have died during physical activity (whether it's running or another sport) had a pre-existing heart condition, either known or unknown, that made them much more susceptible to a cardiac event. It may not be reassuring to runners to learn that they may be carrying ticking time bombs in their chests, so doctors recommend being screened for your risk factor for heart disease. An assessment takes into account family history, cholesterol levels and other indicators.

Unfortunately, some people ignore the warning signs. Doctors say too many people who exercise don't look for indicators of a future heart problem, like tightness in the chest or arms. They dismiss what could be a precursor of a heart attack.

It's also not a good idea to rush into things. While it makes for a nice story to hear that someone has gone from being fifty pounds overweight to running their first marathon in three months, that's riskier than someone who eases into the sport gradually.

It's worth pointing out that running can mask a deeper problem. George Sheehan, a legendary figure in running, once pointed out that there's a difference between being fit and being healthy. Runners may be thin and feel fit, but by burning thousands of extra calories a week, they may be covering up bad eating habits that are contributing to heart disease. If you want to avoid problems, a good diet is critical.

Is it a coincidence that all three people who died in the Detroit half-marathon were men? Probably not, according to Ottawa physician Dr. Barry Dworkin. Because women typically develop cardiovascular disease ten years later in life, and the bulk of the running population is in their thirties and forties, most women who run marathons are less likely to suffer a heart attack than the men in the same race.

Marathons are actually bad for your heart, but only temporarily. Researchers in Winnipeg discovered that, just like your legs, your heart gets injured during a marathon. According to the scientists, the right side of your heart doesn't pump and function as efficiently after a long-distance race. But within a week, it's back to normal. Dr. Paul Thompson, an avid runner and director of cardiology at Hartford Hospital, told Runner's World that, while running a marathon, the risk of a dying from a heart attack roughly doubles for people who exercise regularly and goes up by thirty to fifty times for "weekend warrior types" who exercise less frequently. But most people in both groups start out with a pretty low chance of a cardiac event, so even the increased risk is pretty small.

And remember, even if it causes some temporary damage, running is good for your heart. Notwithstanding the increased risk of a heart attack during a race, regular exercise still decreases your chances of heart disease. Dr. Thompson says that regular exercise creates a thirty to fifty per cent lower overall risk for heart attacks. So while you expose yourself to an increased risk by doing a marathon, you also improve your health by being a runner.

For non-runners, stories about heart attacks may be a convenient excuse to make the sport seem unsafe. But the evidence shows running causes far more benefit than harm.

[FIT AND FACING THE WORLD]

iRun at 50 years old because at 43 I couldn't PETER CICALO, ONTARIO

Somewhere in the throngs of runners stretching down every street in the little town of Hopkinton, Massachusetts stood seventy-five-year-old Alan Rushforth of Ottawa.

A forty-two-kilometre route leading to a finish line in downtown Boston lay ahead of him. But the path behind him was even longer, stretching back to a day about six years earlier when he stood outside a Running Room store in suburban Ottawa, wondering whether or not he should go in.

"When you get to the start line, and they make the announcement that it's the 112th running of the Boston Marathon," says Rushforth, "it's quite a big moment. It's an amazing point in one's life to get there. It ranks up there among the big days, like getting married and dying."

Not that he would know much about the latter. Rushforth's daughter figures running has added some fifteen years to her father's life. And it's made his life better, not just longer.

"If you're with people who are doing things and are active, it helps so much," says Rushforth. "Compared with being around all these people who are talking about dying and who's going next."

Which is where this story begins. Rushforth was a runner in

his late forties and even completed two marathons. But he gave up running when life got too busy. More than twenty years later, something spurred him to take it up again at the age of sixty-nine.

"I went to two reunions," he says. "These were people I'd worked with, people I expected to find quite active and alive like they used to be. Instead, it was rather depressing.

"At the same time I'd seen these groups going out on Sunday mornings, so I decided to creep off and join them."

But when he showed up for his first running clinic, he hesitated.

"I wondered how I would fit in, being as old as I was," he says. "So I waited outside for ten minutes before I plucked up the courage. Finally, I saw someone else go in with grey hair and I followed him in. As soon as I got in there, I was really welcomed and things have gone very well ever since."

Rushforth ran a few half-marathons and even a marathon in 2004, but when arthritis started advancing on him, his doctors advised him to take up another sport. He joined one of the walking groups, but it didn't satisfy him as much as running did.

When he had the chance to ask Running Room founder John Stanton for advice, Stanton advised him to try running again, but to stick to shorter distances. Despite the arthritis, the running went well and before Rushforth knew it, he was doing another half-marathon.

"The arthritis is staying level now," he says. "It's not getting any worse. The running is keeping it at bay."

Rushforth's training group had their eyes set on running the Chicago Marathon, so he tagged along for the long runs, thinking he would split off and do another half-marathon. But the training runs went well and he entered the Niagara Marathon and qualified for Boston.

In April 2008, Rushforth was the only Canadian in the seventy-five-and-over category in Boston. He ran the whole route – scrapping his usual walk breaks even on Heartbreak Hill – and finished in a time of five hours and fifteen minutes.

But it wasn't the finish line that he will remember most, but the start in Hopkinton.

"It makes a day that you can remember forever," he says. "The start line represented the reward for all the hard hill work and training in the winter and all the things I'd been doing.

"It's so much in contrast to everyday life."

When he returned home from Boston, a small group was waiting for him at the airport, including some of the younger runners he'd trained with. A small celebration followed.

For anyone who thinks they couldn't take up running in their late sixties, Rushforth has a simple message: "Get out there and try it," he says.

"Nothing tastes as good as feeling fit. If you're fit, you can face the world, you've got confidence and life is fuller. There are so many benefits there."

$$\left[\text{ MY LIFE AS A BUNNY } \right]$$

iRun to keep up SHAWNA WOLFF, ALBERTA

It's amazing how conspicuous you are when you walk through downtown on a Sunday morning with pink rabbit ears on your head.

When you show up for a major race as an ordinary runner, you're virtually anonymous. The streets are crawling with people like you. However, put on a hat with bunny ears and suddenly you're a minor celebrity, the centre of attention.

In May 2007, for the first time, I served as one of the pace bunnies for a half-marathon. From the time I parked my car until I started driving home, I was never lonely. Before the race started, people pointed at me and smiled, some checking the pace time I had written on my ears and repeating it out loud. "There's the guy you need to follow," I heard one runner say to another.

The next time I was a pace bunny, I was asked to pose for a picture with a young girl who wanted to wear my hat. I dropped to one knee to get to her level but then, seeing what I had done, she kneeled down as well.

In the half-hour before the race, my fellow pace bunny Bob and I were asked a half-dozen random questions about the event: How does the timing chip work? Where do I go for my race number? Which way to the start line? As pace bunnies, we obviously looked more official than other runners, but I still thought it was kind of amusing that people figured the people to trust would be the guys wearing pink ears.

(Bob told me that when he arrived home from the race expo with his ears, his two-year-old daughter said, "Daddy, you've been doing crafts.")

When we got to the start line, a woman behind me said, "I'm going to stick to you for the entire race." About two kilometres in, she proved she meant it when she bumped into me on a turn. A few minutes later, though, she went off ahead of the group, and I didn't see her again until the finish line.

An experienced pace bunny told me the toughest thing about the job was leaving behind the runners who fell off the pace you were setting. "Don't look back," he said. "It's like leaving a lost puppy in the road."

After four or five kilometres, we started to get to know some of the runners in our group, many of whom were from out of town. The most inspiring thing was hearing from runners doing their first half-marathon. They were putting some faith in us to help make it happen, which gave me a little extra incentive to finish on time.

I talked a few times to a runner from Montreal who was doing his very first race. At about seventeen kilometres, I checked how he was doing. "OK," he said, "but, in another few minutes, I'm going to hop on your back."

Even though it was raining, there were thousands of people along the route. "Go, pace bunny!" a lot of spectators shouted. It's hard to miss the pink ears in a sea of other runners. Young children also seemed to enjoy seeing adults wearing rabbit ears, even if they didn't understand why we were doing it.

Bob overheard one spectator on a cellphone, apparently talking to a runner. "The pace bunny just passed us," she said. "Pick it up."

Despite the fact that we were required to take a one-minute walk break for every ten minutes we ran, we maintained a pretty steady pace. The only other minor inconvenience was carrying the sign with our time on it. "Is it hard holding that sign while you're running?" one runner asked me. "Would you like to try?" I asked. She declined.

The odd thing about being a pace bunny is that after leading your charges through the race for more than twenty kilometres, you hope to finish with no one from your group behind you. We encouraged everyone to pour it on in the final kilometre. "I'm going to head off," one runner said, giving me a high five as he sped up.

The final few hundred metres of a race are always a thrill. I looked around for my friend from Montreal, though, and couldn't find him. I was worried he'd fallen behind.

Once we crossed the finish line, we got handshakes and thanks from the members of our group. I waited to see if the runner from Montreal came across the finish line behind us, but I never saw him.

Twenty minutes later, in the recovery area, he came up to me. "Did you make it?" I asked. "Oh yeah," he said. "I went ahead of you guys with a few kilometres left and I finished about a minute before you."

I was already pretty satisfied after running a good race and leading a fun group of runners to the finish line, but hearing that made me a very happy bunny.

iRun to inspire my kids GREG SHAW, ONTARIO

⌈ THE NEXT GENERATION ⌉

No elite international athletes in this field, just a quick young man who somehow finished thirteen seconds ahead of everyone else.

No chase for a world record, either. No high-profile gender challenge, no pace vehicle tracking the leaders, no water stations, no official pace bunnies (except for a grown-up dressed in a rabbit suit).

If you care only about your own fitness, there's nothing in this for you. But if are hopeful that this sport will grow, that the current running boom won't bust – heck, even if you just want kids to be active, then this is the most inspiring event you could watch.

It's certainly the coolest innovation for race organizers since computer-chip timing replaced the volunteers with clipboards. Those events that have taken on a kids' race as one of their activities are growing a new generation of runners.

Is it exciting to watch an elite field compete in a 10k? Sure. But that's nothing like watching 1,200 kids raise their hands and stretch and shout just minutes before the start of the Ottawa Kids Marathon, as I did in 2010. Somewhere in that crowd was the ten-year-old girl who had recently put up *Twilight* posters all over the walls of what used to be my home office.

Is it inspiring to watch runners of all ages, shapes and sizes cross the finish line in the half-marathon and marathon, some of them running on behalf of an important cause, others just achieving a lifelong goal? Sure, but what's that compared to a sea of purple shirts sprinting boldly down the street, with parents running alongside, simultaneously shouting encouragement and recording video.

The Kids Marathon, which was added to the Ottawa event two years ago, was brilliantly conceived. It helps school children get active, set goals, stay in shape and learn about running. The kids run the same distance as a marathon, just spread out over the weeks and months leading up to race day. Then, on the same morning as the marathon, they run the final 1.2k on race day, crossing the same finish line as the adult runners from Kenya to Kamloops, and they walk off with medals and beaming parents.

At some schools, it's quickly become a part of the culture. David Dazé, a teacher and marathon runner at Monsignor Paul Baxter School in suburban Ottawa, leads a group of more than 100 children preparing for the Kids Marathon.

"As soon as I heard about it I thought, I'm signing up my school," says Dazé, a Grade-5 teacher who has done more than a dozen marathons. "I brought all my medals in. I brought in the foil blanket they wrap you in at the end of the race."

Dazé went to every classroom between grades 3 and 6. He figured he might get a few dozen kids to sign up for the race, a new feature of the Ottawa Race Weekend.

"I said to my wife, if I get thirty, that would be great," says Dazé. "But it just sort of exploded."

For some kids, it's personal, starting either with a parent who's into running or just a decision to go after a goal. When she was nine years old, Zoe Ivan learned about fitness and decided she wanted to try running. Her mother, Shirley, helped her map out a 100-metre route for her in the school yard and she ran it five times almost every school day. Zoe finished her marathon in Ottawa with a 1.2k run in a little less than ten minutes.

The Kids Marathon has transformed running into a sport that's truly for everyone. Most race events used to be dominated by people aged thirty and older. Doing a marathon or a 10k just wasn't something the average eighteen- to twenty-four-year-old had the inclination to do. More likely, you came to running to reclaim something you lost: either a notch or two on your belt buckle or a few minutes of alone time in a busy life at home and at work.

But if children are introduced to running at a younger age, some of them might stick with it through their teenage years. Could it be that we're on the verge of a running boom of teenagers and twentysomethings?

This isn't just about boosting the numbers for annual running events. It might also help produce better long-distance runners to compete internationally.

Ken Parker, the coach and former race director, has asked for years why a boom in the running population hasn't yielded more and faster elite runners in Canada. Maybe it's because the growth so far has been fuelled by a lot of runners in their thirties and forties. If more young people are running, we might find more elite athletes, finally break some longstanding records and send some marathon runners to the Olympics again.

The organizers of Ottawa Race Weekend and the other events that have added a kids' marathon haven't just found a way to be more inclusive and boost participation numbers. They might just also be spawning a new generation of runners. Not to mention proud parents and teachers.

Unfortunately, despite inspiring more than 100 kids to run the marathon, Dazé wasn't able to see any of the children cross the finish line. He was too busy running the marathon himself.

[THE COLDEST DAY OF THE YEAR]

iRun because Mother Nature dares me not to JILL SEYMOUR, ALBERTA

There are icicles on my eyelashes.

There are icicles on the icicles on my eyelashes.

This is what happens when your running buddy e-mails you and suggests an early-morning jog on the coldest day of the year. It's hard to say no without feeling like you're being a wimp. So on a Tuesday morning at 7:30, when it was minus-26 and minus-42 with the windchill, I went for a run.

I run four or five times a week right through the winter, but this windchill reading called for special measures. I hunted through several drawers to find longer, thicker socks and a pair of gloves that fit nicely underneath the mitts I usually wear. I dug out a pair of track pants to wear over my normal winter running tights. I pulled out my extra-thick jersey, to wear on top of my regular winter running shirt.

When you're a guy running in the winter, there are three areas of the body you worry about: one is your head, the second is your feet and the third is halfway in between. Before most winter runs, I usually check the temperature and the windchill and assess whether it will be a one-underwear or two-underwear run. (If you make the wrong decision, your only recourse is to sacrifice one of your hands and use a glove for extra protection.)

On this day, there was no debate: double-underwear.

I covered my ears with a headband, pulled a hat over that and then put a balaclava around my neck and brought it up to cover my face. The only area of skin showing on my entire body was a small area around my eyes. I was perfectly dressed for a winter run or a bank job.

I left the house just as my friend was arriving. As we started our run, most of my body felt well protected; in fact, I felt better than on slightly warmer winter days when I've been wearing less clothing. I had three layers on my upper body, two on my legs and four in the middle. Not even this level of punishing cold could get through all of that.

But the bitter wind found its way to my two most vulnerable areas. My feet were starting to feel like I'd just put them in the freezer. And when the air hit my eyes, they started to ache in a way I've rarely felt before. I started wondering if it was possible to get frostbite on your eyeballs.

I did my best to duck into the wind and shield my eyes with my hand, moving it out of the way every few seconds to see where I was going. I brought my hat down as low as it could go without covering my eyes. My toes started to ache. Running shoes are designed to vent heat, not retain it. For my next run, I decided, I would wear two pairs of socks.

We changed directions and found that somehow the wind was still in our faces. But within five minutes, I was feeling warm everywhere except my eyes and toes. I actually may have started to sweat.

Two kilometres into the run, we passed a guy who was biking to work. If you think running in winter weather is crazy, I would point you in this fellow's direction. You don't know what windchill is until you've been on a bicycle in winter. (A few days later, I heard a rumour that someone had been seen that day in my neighbourhood, biking in shorts and a T-shirt. I have a hard time buying that story, but two people swore it was true.)

We passed a few well-bundled pedestrians who were shuffling off to the bus stop or the office. I don't remember encountering any other runners, but I know from experience there were others out there, all over the city.

After another ten minutes, I noticed my toes weren't sore anymore. I wasn't sure if that was a good sign or a bad one. By now, the moisture was freezing in clumps on my eyelashes. I glanced at my friend and saw little bits of ice forming all over his hat and balaclava.

I figure it was probably on a day like this that the treadmill was invented. Our only consolation was a weather forecast that called for warmer temperatures ahead.

"In two weeks, we could be running in shorts," my friend said.

I could be doing that right now if I'd just gone to the gym, I thought.

By the time I dropped my friend at his house and headed for home, the only inconvenience was that the icicles were making it hard to open and close my eyes. Now that I was warmed up, it felt like any other winter run. And it was a nice, bright sunny day. I could actually go another kilometre, I thought as I turned down my street.

But the warmth of my house was too much to resist. I went inside to check on my toes and melt the ice from my eyes.

Within a few days, it was warm enough that I was running in freezing rain. Some weeks, you wear a different amount of clothing for almost every run.

I wouldn't want to run in minus-42 windchill every day, but once in a while is enough to make me feel like I've conquered winter.

[LADIES FIRST IN BOSTON]

iRun to reach my goals KERRY KENNEDY, ONTARIO

My next-door neighbour runs about as fast (or as slow) as I do, so we make good training partners. We've run with each other often. Still, we'll probably never enter the Boston Marathon together.

Even though we run at roughly the same pace – in fact, my fastest marathon time is even a bit faster – a few years ago my neighbour was on the verge of qualifying for Boston, whereas I was still a whopping twenty-five minutes off the required time.

Why is a runner of equal speed almost a half-hour closer to the Holy Grail of marathons? Because my next-door neighbour is a woman.

At any given time, tens of thousands of runners across the world are training with the goal of qualifying for Boston, but not everyone gets an equal chance at what many runners consider to be the dream of a lifetime.

Forty years ago, the Boston Marathon banned women completely. Today, it's the opposite. I think the Boston qualifying times discriminate against men.

Even when she was in her twenties, my neighbour was knocking on Boston's door while she was still in the age group with the toughest qualifying time. If she didn't make it right away, she was destined to eventually, as an extra five minutes would be added with each age milestone she hit.

When I was in my thirties, however, I had two ways to qualify for Boston: either shave more than twenty minutes off my time (thirty seconds per kilometre for forty-two consecutive kilometres) or keep running at the same speed until I was in my mid-fifties. To do either without help from Barry Bonds' trainer seemed highly improbable.

Qualifying times were introduced to the Boston Marathon in 1970. If you can believe it, it's because race organizers felt the field, which was about 1,100 the previous year, was getting too big and unmanageable. Now, the race is bursting with more than 25,000 runners and they've had to make the test for entering increasingly difficult.

The original qualifying time was four hours. That didn't do anything to stem the number of starters, so six years later the organizers cut the qualifying time dramatically: to 3:00 for men and 3:30 for women and men over forty. In the years that followed, organizers have tinkered with the qualifying times half a dozen times.

Today, there is a sliding scale based on age. If you're a man aged eighteen to thirty-four, you have to run a 3:10 marathon to get into Boston. If you're a woman over eighty, all you have to do is run 42.2 kilometres in five-and-a-half hours and you're in.

In 2012, the times will get even tougher, by five minutes per age group. But one thing won't change. Over the course of thirty-five years of fine-tuning the requirements, there has been a strange constant: in every age group, women get an extra half-hour.

Fine, you might say. On average, women don't run as fast as men. So they shouldn't have the same qualifying times.

Fair enough. Why half an hour, though? What's the logic behind that? Where's the scientific evidence that women run, on average, thirty minutes slower than men, no matter what age category?

There is none. The gap is mostly arbitrary, and illogical, especially when women get the same thirty minutes no matter what age group. A thirty-minute advantage is a lot bigger in a 3:40 marathon than one that takes 4:30.

The fastest male and female runners in the world certainly aren't half an hour apart anymore. In 1970, the women's world record in the marathon was fifty minutes slower than the men's. When Paula Radcliffe set a new women's world record in 2003, it was less than ten minutes slower than the men's record at the time.

If Boston qualifying times were completely fair, the same proportion of men and women would run Boston as any other marathon. However, Boston has a much higher percentage of women participants than any other major marathon. Women make up two out of every five runners in the starting field in Boston, whereas the New York marathon, as one example, is closer to thirty per cent women.

If, to Boston Marathon organizers, the idea of equality is to have a disproportionate number of women in the field, then they should consider skewing the qualifying times even further so that women make up fifty per cent of the field.

Still, if they want qualifying for Boston to continue to be the ultimate achievement for all amateur marathoners, they should adjust the times so they're based more on data and less on an arbitrary gap of thirty minutes. Qualifying for Boston should be equally hard for men and women, not more favourable to one group over the other.

[ALWAYS A RUNNER]

iRun to see how far I've come MASTER CORPORAL PAUL FRANKLIN

For Master Corporal Paul Franklin, a 600-metre walk in May 2006 was tougher than any marathon.

After losing both his legs in Afghanistan, Franklin vowed one day he would take his son Simon to class again.

"I thought, it doesn't matter how long it takes, one day I would like to walk my son to school," says Franklin. "Even if it's to college."

The short walk took forty-five minutes. "It was exhausting," says Franklin.

But it was a vital step in a recovery that transformed Franklin's life.

In 2006, Franklin was a runner who had completed the Dubai Marathon and four Mountain Man Challenges, a military competition in which soldiers run for three kilometres, canoe for ten kilometres and run another seven kilometres to the finish line.

"Everybody (in the military) is a runner," says Franklin. "Most don't like it, but I did. It's the knowledge that you're doing something more than other people can do. When you've finished it, you've accomplished something to be proud of. I remember the first time I ran 20k, I was so proud of myself."

A year after completing Dubai, Franklin was driving a vehicle into Kandahar that was struck by a suicide attacker.

"My truck jumped about ten metres in the air and twenty feet across the road and landed on its side. My left leg was torn off immediately. My right leg was destroyed."

Franklin's goal during treatment was to run again. But he soon learned that running on prosthetics would be very difficult for someone who lost both legs above the knee.

"I had it in my head that I had to learn to run again," he says. "I wanted to recover to the person I was. What I discovered was that person was dead.

"The moment I realized that I could never run again was the moment I realized that the person I used to be was dead and gone. I had to change my attitude. I had to have other challenges."

Franklin does use prosthetic legs for walking, during transit and when he's doing public speaking. "They allow me to pee standing up, which is an amazing thing," he says.

But he spends most of his time in a wheelchair. In September 2008, he raced the 5k in the first Army Run in Ottawa. A number of injured soldiers competed in the event, which raised money for Soldier On, a program which helps with rehabilitation.

"For me it was nice to get back into running," he says. "Even though it's in a wheelchair, I still consider it running. It was a feeling that I was back into running."

Franklin says he doesn't train like he used to because being in a wheelchair is almost enough training on its own.

"There's so much strength needed to just get yourself around," he says. "It's pretty shocking sometimes just how much effort this whole thing is."

Still a member of the Canadian Forces, Franklin now works in casualty support in Edmonton. "As wounded soldiers come back, we try and help them out and try and make their lives a little bit better," he says.

He tells other wounded soldiers to learn from his experience the day he realized he would never run again.

"A lot of people struggle to return to who they were before. But that person doesn't exist anymore," he says. "The sooner you can accept that, the sooner you can move on with your life."

But even though he's accepted that he will never run again on two legs, Franklin still considers himself a runner.

"I definitely think of myself as a runner. That allowed me to be the person I am today. My runner's body – being fit – is what saved my life in Kandahar. If I had not been fit, I would not have been able to recover as quickly.

"I'll always be a runner. Even if it's in a wheelchair. It will always be a piece of me."

[THE TOP OF THE WORLD: FLAT BUT STEEP]

iRun because it's opened up another world for me KELLI CATANA, ONTARIO

By the time April rolls around, have you had enough of winter? Or, rather than running in shorts as spring arrives, would you prefer to be putting on layer over layer, still finishing your long runs with icicles on your earlobes?

Then maybe the North Pole Marathon is for you. Picture yourself on top of the world, basking in the twenty-four-hour sunshine while you complete ten laps of a 4.2-kilometre course somewhere between 89 and 90 degrees north.

That's what anywhere from twenty-five to forty runners from a dozen countries do every April. They join a short but growing list of athletes who have raced in what the *Guinness Book of World Records* has declared the world's northernmost marathon.

Looking for a unique race experience? What other marathon lists as one of the frequently asked questions on its website, "Will there be a threat from polar bears?"

The answer: "It would be highly unusual for a polar bear to travel that far north, though the camp operators keep weapons for such an eventuality. To date, no marathoner has seen a polar bear on the trip!" In other words, not even the polar bears are that crazy.

Race organizers call the event the world's coolest marathon.

Although the course is pretty flat, it may also be the steepest marathon on the planet, thanks to the entry fee of just under 12,000 euros (roughly $16,000). And that doesn't include making – and paying – your own way to the expedition gathering point in Spitsbergen, a sparsely populated Norwegian island in the Arctic Sea that makes Baffin Island look like Manhattan.

A magazine review once called it a "priceless adventure" but that's not exactly true. It makes you wonder what is the more gruelling test: running the race or writing the cheque.

In return for the price of a new car, runners are flown two-and-a-half hours by converted Russian cargo plane from Spitsbergen to Barneo, a camp near the geographic North Pole. The day after arrival, they race over snow and ice, with windchill temperatures dipping to as low as minus-forty. In other words, just like January in Canada.

As if the experience of running near the North Pole isn't unique enough, the race is believed to be the only marathon run entirely off land. The runners actually race on a giant Arctic ice floe, six to twelve feet thick.

And while the runners won't be able to tell, the course will be drifting the entire time they are running. No two loops will be run in the same geographic position.

"The ice is quite robust," one of the organizers said about the race a few years ago. Good to know, considering there's 3,600 metres of Arctic Sea below it.

When the race is over, the runners take a helicopter to the geographic North Pole, where they stand on top of the world for a few minutes before boarding the cargo plane back to civilization. Well, at least to Spitsbergen.

The race was started by Irishman Robert Donovan, who ran

42.2 kilometres on the Arctic ice by himself in 2002 and decided to invite a few friends to join him the next year. The race became an annual event and so far, about 200 have completed the distance, including legendary British explorer Sir Ranulph Fiennes and Irish author Michael Collins.

The race distance is certified by international authorities, but thanks to the uneven terrain, it's not likely to produce a Boston-qualifying result for everyone. The course record is 3:36 but many years the winning time is over five hours.

Of course, conditions vary widely from year to year, but to give you an idea of what the footing is like, the *New York Times* reported one year that three entrants were preparing by running in snowshoes on the beach at Coney Island. One of them also travelled to Winnipeg in January to get a feel for what Arctic weather would be like. Close enough.

Travelling to the North Pole to run a marathon can give you a new perspective. If nothing else, it might make the entry fee for a North American marathon seem cheap.

[A DETOUR ON THE WAY TO BOSTON]

iRun for those who cannot BRIAN TAYLOR, ONTARIO

It all goes back to one run.

There are the 17,000 students who have been inspired by the story, the thousands of dollars already raised, the $500,000 goal for the next five years, the dozens of people who ran Ottawa Race Weekend in support of the cause and the most inspiring race-day aid station you could ever imagine.

And all of that goes back to one run.

The run was one day after Shelby Hayter found out she had Parkinson's disease. Picture being a month away from the Boston Marathon – for which you actually had to be pretty fast to qualify – and you've just learned your body is slowing down, much more quickly than it should.

Hayter wouldn't have been training for Boston if it wasn't for her sister, Andrea. And that's where the story really begins. Andrea Mozas was recovering from a brain tumour in 2004 and decided she wanted to run a marathon with her sister. Hayter, who's been a runner since she was thirteen, had completed a marathon when she was twenty and thought at the time, "I've checked that one off my list."

She didn't think she would ever run a marathon again. Good thing she was wrong.

"When she said, 'I want to run a marathon with you,' my reaction was, 'Oh no you don't,'" says Hayter, a mother of three. "But then I said, 'OK, I'll do it with you.' Because she's my little sister and she had been so brave.

"I'll do one. But that's it."

Wrong again.

Mozas and Hayter ran the marathon in Toronto in 2004 and qualified for Boston. So of course they had to run that together, too. And it was on a training run in the winter of 2005 that Hayter noticed something was wrong.

"That's when I noticed the slightest of discrepancies," says Hayter. "On my left-hand side I felt there was a weightedness. Just like there was a one- or two-pound weight on my left hand or my left foot."

After a series of tests, the doctors gave her the news that would change her life. And the next day she went for the run that would change thousands of others.

From that run came the idea to do Boston as a fundraiser for Parkinson's research. Her doctor cleared her to run, so Hayter came up with the slogan "Twenty-six miles for Boston, one cure for Parkinson's" and raised $36,000. From that Boston effort came a lot of media attention and a proposal from a total stranger. Tracy Tremble, a runner from Montreal who had Parkinson's in her family and had read about Hayter, knocked on her door one day. Tremble suggested they put a team together to run the Ottawa half-marathon in 2006. They raised another $9,000.

The next year, the team of runners grew and Tremble suggested recruiting more volunteers to staff an aid station along the route.

"We had a sea of red shirts and they all said 'Team Parkinson's,'" says Hayter. "What touched me the most was that amongst the people were the researchers, the neurologists and their families. There were friends of mine handing out sponges. My family was handing out sponges. There were about forty of them. I ran up to them and I thought, 'if this is not a fantastic example of community spirit and compassion, I don't know what is.'"

Along the way, Hayter also started speaking in schools with a program called Pass the Baton for Parkinson's. She tells kids about the disease, takes them for a run around the gym and encourages them to donate and raise money and tell others about it as well.

And then a group of investment bankers, all with friends or family who have been affected by Parkinson's, approached the Ottawa Hospital Foundation. They ran Ottawa Race Weekend under the name Partners Investing in Parkinson's Research, and they set a goal of raising $500,000 over five years, all for groundbreaking work at The Ottawa Hospital Research Institute.

"They have significant goals," says Hayter. "And they've got influence in the city. And they've got enthusiasm. And it brings us to a whole new level."

Hayter deflects questions about her health, saying, "I don't have time to think about it." But she admits she suffers tremors on her left side and she doesn't run as well as she used to.

"I've always run with such ease and with a confident stride. Now I'm noticing that, physically and mentally, it's way more challenging to get out the door and pound the pavement. But all this community support – it fuels me and humbles me and puts a drive in my stride."

In 2009, Hayter was still running three times a week and she ran the 10k at Ottawa Race Weekend, along with her husband and one of her kids. Then all five members of the family showed up the next day to work the sponge station for the marathon.

And all of this – the children's program, the inspired volunteers, the thousands of dollars for research, the aid station – because in March 2005, one day after learning she had Parkinson's disease, Shelby Hayter went for a run. She could have chosen not to run. She could have spent the run feeling sorry for herself. She could have thought about the dramatic turn her life had suddenly taken.

Instead, she made a decision to turn her bad news into something positive.

"When I came back in the door, I said to my husband, 'I've got this idea.' He looked at me and he said, 'Let's do it.'

"The fact that I got diagnosed one month before Boston was almost lucky in a strange way," she says, "because it allowed my story to begin."

[A NEW WAY TO COMMUTE]

iRun to discover the things I drive past too quickly JOANNA SCHULTZ, ONTARIO

It felt like the finish line to a marathon. And, in a way, it was.

In 2009, during a long transit strike, I ran back and forth almost every weekday to do my radio show.

At the end of each week, I felt I was completing an endurance event spread over five days. When I reached my doorstep, I felt a mixture of satisfaction and relief. And a little bit of pain in my hamstrings and some numbness in my toes. But I didn't take very long to celebrate. I went inside and started peeling off the layers.

On one level, it was no big deal: a series of relatively short runs. On another, it was gruelling. Ten runs in five days, back and forth along the same mostly uninspiring route. And for three of those days, I ran through the coldest temperatures of the winter.

In a one-car family, this is what it took to get around when the buses – and the opposing sides in the dispute – were showing no signs of movement.

Fortunately, I live only slightly more than five kilometres from downtown, but that still adds up to more than fifty-two kilometres spread over five days.

Considering my normal training routine might be three midweek runs of about eight kilometres each, it was more than twice my normal distance without a lot of rest. It's very unusual for me to run more than two or three days without a day off, and I'm pretty sure I've never run more than ten kilometres a day for five straight days.

Early in the week, my commute was uneventful. Then came the forecast for Wednesday, Thursday and Friday. Temperatures below minus-twenty and wind chills down to minus-thirty-nine. On Wednesday, I briefly considered taking a cab and then figured: if Ray Zahab can run every day in Antarctica, I can handle Ottawa.

On the first day of the deep freeze, I was actually overdressed. I wore three shirts underneath a protective shell, two layers on my legs, extra thick socks, a pair of gloves under my mitts, a headband underneath my hat and a facemask that left only my eyes exposed. All in, it was about five pounds of clothing. And by the time I got to work, I was actually sweaty.

For the rest of the week, I wore one fewer layer on top and my body never once felt cold. Once in a while, my thumbs got a bit numb, so I tucked them in to the main part of the glove until they warmed up.

Only my toes felt like they could use more protection, but I couldn't squeeze another layer of socks into my shoes.

Along the way, I discovered, to my surprise, it takes me roughly the same amount of time to get from door-to-door as taking the bus or even driving (and parking and walking). I left my house at the same time every day as I normally would.

And unlike after a vehicular commute, when I got home, my workout was done. So it actually saved me time every day.

But it wasn't the best of running. Except for the downtown portion, the route was boring and very repetitive. And I always ran by myself and missed out on my usual runs (and talks) with my running buddy.

Given that I was running in rush-hour traffic, I didn't think it was safe to listen to music, so the time was quiet. And instead of combining a mixture of training runs, such as hills and tempo runs and intervals, I was doing the same thing over and over. And over and over.

Even on the coldest days, there was a small amount of snow on the sidewalks that made the footing less than ideal.

And that wasn't the only obstacle. Most pedestrians were courteous and kept to one side. But there were a handful who seemed to think the paths were for them alone, walking down the middle and forcing everyone else to move around them.

There was the occasional group of people walking four abreast that didn't move out of the way. I collided with one of them on Friday morning.

Among the few highlights was seeing other hardy runners, cyclists and pedestrians who braved the coldest temperatures the city had to offer, including one man with a giant moustache covered in frost.

And twice a day I could mentally tip my cap to a statue of Terry Fox. Even on the coldest day, that put my little commute in perspective.

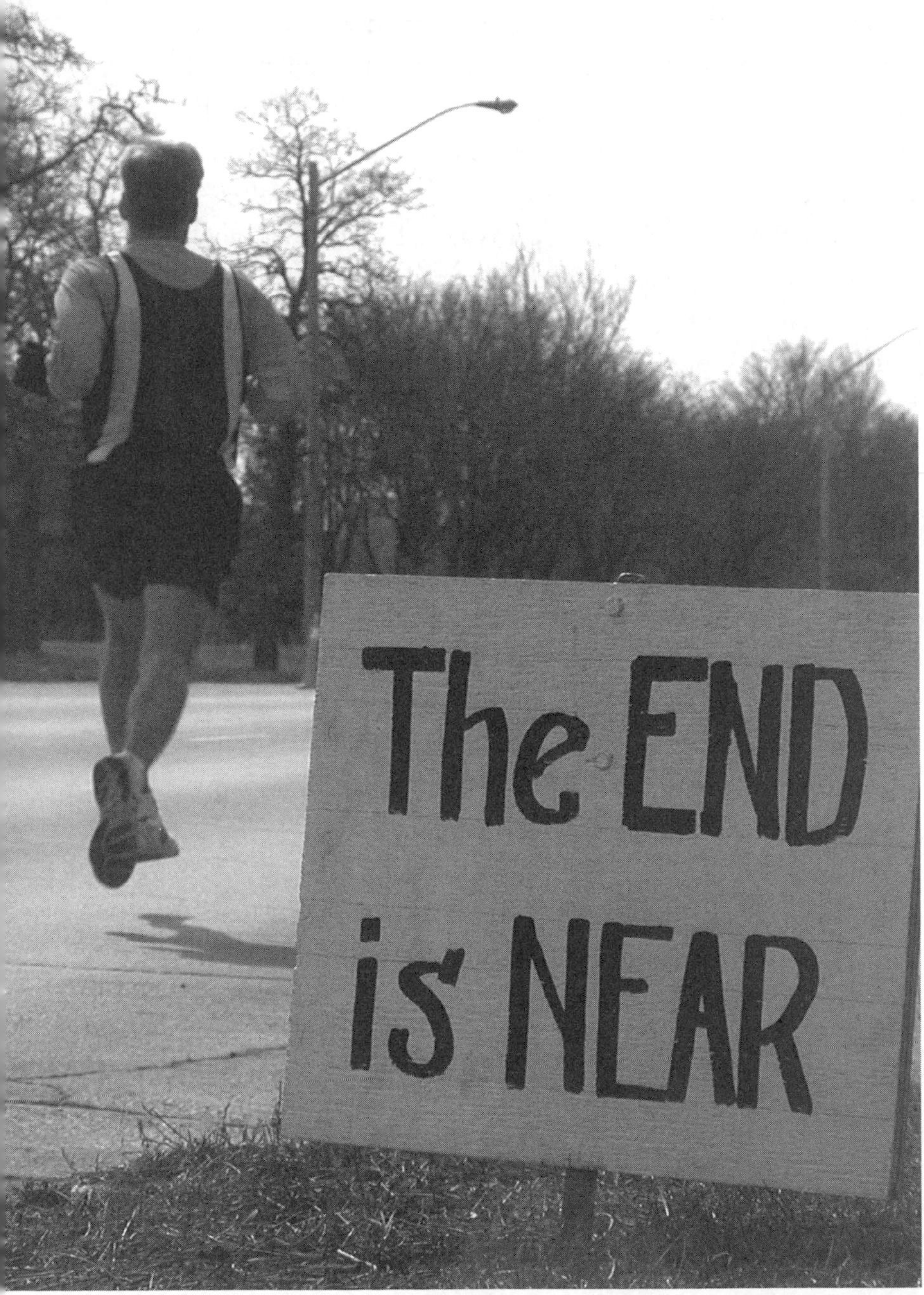
The END
is NEAR

[RUNNING PAST THE GRIM REAPER]

iRun to stay ahead of the Grim Reaper CRAIG BUSHEY, ONTARIO

The oldest footrace in North America is not the legendary Boston Marathon, which was first run in 1897. Rather, it's the challenging 30-kilometre loop through Hamilton and Burlington on the edge of Lake Ontario called Around the Bay.

Around the Bay was first staged on Christmas Day 1894, almost two years before the modern Olympic era began in Athens. Since there was no such thing as the Running Room in those days, the race was sponsored by the owner of a cigar store. First place in a field of thirteen earned Billy Marshall a $25 cup and three boxes of stogies.

Archival photos from the early years show the leaders following a pace car that is actually a horse-drawn carriage.

Because it's not a marathon or a big-city event, Around the Bay doesn't have the profile of Boston. This is more of a people's race, with a blue-collar feel in keeping with its Steeltown roots.

Over the years, though, the race has drawn its share of stars, including a short list of runners who won both Around the Bay and Boston in the same year, such as Canadians Jack Caffrey and Tom Longboat.

It would be nice to think the race was founded purely out of 19th-century athletic ideals, but one of the big attractions for early spectators was wagering. Longboat was a 100-to-1 longshot when he won in 1906.

The gambling component is gone, though the rich but understated history of the event makes it a big draw today for runners from all over Eastern Canada and the Northeastern United States. It's also the first long-distance run of the spring in this part of the continent, and the race is particularly popular as a tune-up race for anyone training for a May marathon.

Around the Bay may be twelve kilometres shorter than a marathon, but that doesn't mean the course is easy. The race starts and ends in downtown Hamilton and loops counter-clockwise around Hamilton Harbour. At about the halfway point, with Lake Ontario stretching to the right, the course crosses the small lift bridge that stands in the shadow of the Skyway Bridge.

The first twenty kilometres are fairly flat; the next ten more than make up for that. Through the western part of Burlington, the course goes up and down five or six rolling hills, until it turns back into Hamilton. To punctuate the toughest stretch of the course, on the last of the steep hills, there is a man dressed as the Grim Reaper standing outside the Hamilton Cemetery.

"At this point in the race, people are feeling absolutely crappy," the Grim Reaper told me in 2008. "So this gives them something to look forward to. A little bit of humour. Especially after that hill. That hill is absolutely horrible. This stretch along here, it's close to three kilometres leading up to this hill and after running all that other stuff, it makes you feel like you're dead."

The Reaper tries to stay until the last runner goes by, saying he's there for the people in the middle to the back of the pack, the ones who will feel the most "dead" by the time they reach him.

"Some people are afraid to touch me," he says. "By the end of the day, I have very sore hands because a lot of people come and give me high fives. But some people go as far away as possible. A lot of people say, 'Not this year.' I say, 'Just wait. You haven't gotten to the finish line yet.'"

Once in a while, a labouring runner will choose to stop and perhaps even sit down near the Grim Reaper.

"I'll go over and try to walk them into the cemetery. I'll say, 'If you're ready,'" he says. "Nobody's collapsed in front of me yet. I'm waiting for the year that (someone) will."

Around the Bay is about more than just running thirty kilometres and tuning up for a spring marathon. It's about joining a tradition that has spanned three centuries. And about cheating death.

$$\Big[\ \text{JUST BECAUSE}\ \Big]$$

iRun for the moment when both feet are off the ground CATHERINE ANDERSON, BRITISH COLUMBIA

The first rule of training is to have a goal. Working toward a target race can give you a tangible objective, a sense of purpose and help you fight inertia to stay on the couch instead of going out for a run.

But sometimes, running without a goal is a welcome change. Every so often, after a period of one race after another, I find myself in a unique position when I don't know what my next race will be.

So far, on those occasions when I haven't known what I was training for, I was still training. And usually it's been almost as much as I was before. And I've found myself rediscovering why I love running, instead of seeing each run as a step toward race day.

There's nothing wrong with setting a long-term goal, of course. A 10k race or marathon is an important element of training for many athletes. The actual accomplishment is a big part of the appeal, but a target race also provides a really good reason to stick to a training regimen that not only gets you ready for race day, it keeps you in good shape.

Without a goal to work towards, it can be difficult to squeeze exercise into a busy life. There's less incentive to push past a basic level of fitness, beyond a routine half-hour jog. Sometimes it's tough just to get out the door.

But my training has always leaned toward the obsessive. When I prepared for my first marathon, I followed an eighteen-week program with fanatical zeal. I completed almost every single run on the schedule exactly as prescribed, checking each one off as soon as I came back into the house.

In a week where my time was squeezed, training was usually the last thing I sacrificed, at the expense of other activities I wished I was doing more of, like reading or sleeping. I always worried that, if I slipped a little bit, I'd slip a lot.

Sometimes, I've had as many as four events planned out in the future. But on one occasion, I found myself in unfamiliar territory: I had no specific goals for the whole year.

Would I run a spring race? I hadn't decided yet. Was there another marathon in front of me? Probably. I wanted to do another marathon because I thought I had a faster one in me. But at that point, no specific plans.

And yet, I was still running five times a week. Even on a winter trip to South America, I ran about fifty kilometres each week. And on returning to frosty Canada, my training didn't slide, although my feet sometimes did.

On one evening run in Argentina, I realized I was running not because I had to, not because I was working towards a race, but just because I wanted to.

Back in Canada, jogging through an early-morning light snow, that same liberating feeling came over me, a sense that I was enjoying the experience of an individual run, not because it was getting me closer to a long-term goal.

Even when I don't have a goal, it's not like there aren't still motivating factors that push me, for better or for worse. I worry about falling out of shape. The competitive part of me (which part isn't?) doesn't want my fitness to lag behind the people I normally train with. And I'm still compulsive about training even when I don't have a goal. I feel like I'm doing something wrong if I go without it for two or three days.

But mostly during those periods I enjoy the immediate rewards of training instead of the long-term benefits. I savour that healthy feeling that lasts all day, not to mention knowing I can have dessert if I want to.

It never lasts forever; eventually, I pick some races I want to do and start training with them in mind. But I relish the luxury of training without goals. I enjoy the unexpected and unfamiliar activity of running because ... well, just because.

[**FROM A TO Z**]

iRun everywhere LAURA CRANNA, ONTARIO

A is for Amsterdam, where Gavin Lumsden of Ottawa ran a marathon in 2004. And ascent. Just a few months later, he joined an ill-fated attempt to climb Mount Everest that changed his life.

B is for the Berlin Marathon, which Lumsden ran in September 2005. And base camp. On the slopes of Everest, Lumsden found inspiration in tragedy and was driven to seek out a challenge of his own.

C is for Cumberland. And commitment. It was after running the Fall Colours Marathon in Cumberland in October 2005 that Lumsden thought, "Maybe I can finish the whole alphabet." Three-and-a-half years later, he had one letter to go.

D is for the Disney Marathon in 2007. And disease, diabetes and depression, just some of the effects of a sedentary lifestyle, a societal problem Lumsden is trying to combat with his twenty-six marathons.

E is for Edmonton in August 2006. And Dr. Sean Egan, a health and fitness advocate who died trying to become the oldest Canadian to climb Everest. Lumsden is carrying on Egan's mission to promote wellness and carries a photo of him on every marathon he runs.

F is for Flanders, Belgium, where Lumsden ran in 2007. And

Fox. Lumsden carries a commemorative Terry Fox loonie in his right shoe.

G is for Gainesville, Florida, which he ran in February 2009. And Gavin. "But it's not really about me," he protests. "I'm just running. I'm hoping that we'll inspire other people to take action, to take notice of the cause."

H is for Hamilton in 2007. And horrified. Lumsden says he was stunned particularly by the number of Canadian children suffering from obesity.

I is for Inverness, Scotland, in September 2008. And income. Lumsden discovered it's especially hard for parents with limited resources to put their children into activities that keep them fit.

J is for Jacksonville, Florida, in December 2007. And January 2009, when Lumsden launched a website to expand his mission from creating awareness to raising funds, for the Sean Egan Ascent for Kids Endowment.

K is for Kiawah Island, South Carolina, where Lumsden ran a marathon near the end of 2008. And Kids Fit, the YMCA program for which he has been volunteering two nights a week.

L is for London, Ont., in May 2007. And lowering BMI. Lumsden has watched the body-mass index of Kids Fit participants drop, with a corresponding increase in self-esteem.

M is for Miami. And momentum. The Kids Fit program has expanded to several YMCA branches and is currently helping seventy-five local children.

N is for New York, in November 2007. And nutrition. Kids Fit doesn't just help children to be more active, it teaches them to eat healthier.

O is for Ottawa, the last marathon of twenty-six in May 2009. And outliving your parents. The Ontario Medical Association predicts many of today's children won't.

P is for Philadelphia, in November 2007. And peers. In Kids Fit, says Lumsden, everyone is equal, so there's no bullying or teasing.

Q is for Quebec City, in August 2007. And a question: which marathons are Lumsden's favourites so far? Berlin, New York and Flanders.

R is for Rome, in March 2008. And the Running Room, where Lumsden coaches marathon clinics on top of running his own races, all part of his goal of promoting an active lifestyle.

S is for San Francisco in August 2007. And "the smiles on the children's faces," which Lumsden says "are quite simply priceless."

T is for Toronto, in September 2007. And tired. Lumsden admits it was a long journey and no small expense to travel to twenty-six cities in less than five years.

U is for Ucluelet, British Columbia, a scenic island run in June 2007. And unaffordable. Kids Fit costs $278 for a ten-week program, out of reach for many inner-city families. "No child that could possibly benefit from this should go without because they can't afford it," says Lumsden.

V is for Vancouver in May 2007. And vacation time. While maintaining a full-time job at Rogers Television, Lumsden has built a couple of holidays around his races, but most of the time it's been three- or four-day trips, even when flying to Europe and back.

W is for Winnipeg in June 2007. And war. The most moving experience, says Lumsden, was the special welcome he received as a Canadian in the historic battle site of Flanders.

X is for Xenia, Ohio, which Lumsden ran in April 2008. And it's the last letter in the word "twenty-six." Twenty-six marathons, twenty-six miles each. And Lumsden shares a coincidental statistic: twenty-six per cent of Canadian children are overweight and half of those are clinically obese.

Y is for Yonkers in September 2007. And you. Lumsden asked for at least forty-two volunteers to join him in running his last marathon in Ottawa, each with a commitment to raise $1,000 for Ascent for Kids.

Z is for Zurich, in April 2009. And zero. Which is how many marathons Lumsden intended to run after his last one in Ottawa.

[MUSIC TO EVERY RUNNER'S EARS]

iRun because I can't dance MARIO JAVIER, ONTARIO

About thirteen kilometres into a half-marathon, I passed a runner wearing a bright orange shirt and a pair of headphones.

As soon as I was in front of him, he began to shout, "I wanna push you down, well I will, well I will. I wanna take you for granted, I wanna take you for granted, yeah I will, I will."

Either he was listening to the song *Push* by Matchbox 20, or he was talking smack to me. Or maybe it was a combination of the two. A few minutes later, he passed me and I got to watch him pump his fists in the air to his favourite tunes for about three kilometres – and even do a phantom drum solo – before I finally passed him again and left him behind for good.

It's a rare athlete who sings out loud or does air-band routines, but on everything from a short training run to a long-distance race, music can be a lonely runner's best friend.

Music has been part of running since the Walkman was invented thirty years ago. Today, there are portable music devices and headphones designed for and marketed specifically to runners. Dozens of websites are devoted to the quest for the ideal running playlist. One site even lists the beats per second of particular songs, so runners can choose music to match the tempo of the type of workout they want.

Indeed, for some runners, training without an iPod or MP3 player would be like running without shoes. And for competitors in long-distance races, especially those in the middle to the back of the pack, getting through the many hours of a marathon without a little musical accompaniment seems unfathomable.

But running with music has become a subject of fierce debate in the community.

A few years ago, the governing body for long-distance racing in the U.S. issued an outright ban on headphones at races. But in 2008, it backtracked. Now, only elite runners aren't allowed to listen to music. Individual race directors can use their own discretion on the rule for the rest of the field. One marathon that used to ban headphones has already started allowing them again.

The debate surfaced again when someone posted a story on the TriRudy website about encountering a runner with headphones who was oblivious to car traffic. She encouraged race directors to ban headphones for safety reasons. John Halvorsen, the race director for the Ottawa Marathon, replied with his own comments and then he threw out an open-ended comment: "I'm looking forward to more comments from the community on this."

And – what do you know? – he got what he asked for. One runner after another waded into the discussion. Many of them were people who rarely posted comments on any other topic.

"I'm not sure I could run without music," one person wrote.

"No way am I running 21.1k without music to carry me through when it starts to hurt," said another.

A third runner was equally blunt: "I've tried running without music, I hate it."

There were just as many people posting in support of a ban.

"I enjoy running and wonder why people need to distract

themselves to trick themselves through the time," said one runner.

Another pointed out, "There are no other sports where personal music devices are permitted in competition."

I find the level of passion interesting because I am not religious about either side. I used to do the occasional training run with an iPod, but now I usually run without any music other than the song that's stuck in my head. I have run a couple of races wearing earphones but now I prefer not to.

I understand why some people would rather do a solo long run with a soundtrack, to ward off the monotony, just as I accept that others prefer not to. And I also get why a faster runner is annoyed if a slower runner doesn't respond to the sound of approaching footsteps because he can't hear them.

But most of the arguments on both sides are about personal preference, not a legitimate reason for or against a ban. It's a bit ridiculous to say you could never run without music, since it's your legs that are carrying you whether you can hear Coldplay or not. Do yourself a favour: ditch the iPod for one day and give it a try.

Likewise, it's immaterial to suggest that because some people prefer the sounds of their own foot strike and breathing, or there is some therapeutic benefit to silence, that everyone should go without music. I prefer running without headphones because I like to hear what's going on around me. But that doesn't mean I should force everyone else to do the same.

Ultimately, there's only one legitimate basis for deciding whether headphones should be banned or whether they should be a matter of personal choice: safety. And while there are plenty of anecdotal stories about oblivious iPod-impeded runners getting in the way, I have yet to see any concrete evidence that serious harm has befallen a music listener or the victim of one.

I'd advise anyone running with headphones at any time to keep the volume low enough that it's still possible to hear what's happening around you. But I don't see enough evidence to ban them completely. It feels to me like it's more of a pet peeve for the proponents of a ban than a legitimate safety concern. Everyone has a story of an irritation, an annoyance or even a close call, but where is the actual calamity that was caused by someone wearing headphones?

Insurance companies and lawyers are generally a cautious bunch. After one person – the first in seventy-five years – was killed by a flying puck at a National Hockey League game, nets that impaired the view of spectators were installed at every arena. If in these litigious times the governing body in the U.S. is moving away from a headphone ban, and the underwriters of events aren't insisting on one, listening to music can't be that dangerous.

Anytime you put a bunch of people together in a tight space, some of them are going to get in your way, whether they're listening to music or not. Some people are oblivious and inconsiderate even when their ears are wide open.

And in this country, unless there's concrete evidence that a ban will save individuals from serious harm, we let people decide for themselves.

[PLAYING IT SAFE]

iRun hard! iRun safe! ROLAND GERVAIS, ALBERTA

I failed to learn my lesson after a run nearly turned tragic. Instead, I ended up repeating the very same mistake.

On an early-morning run, I approached an intersection of two side streets. I was in the home stretch, just blocks from my house. The end was within reach and I was basking in the pleasure of finishing a good run.

Just as I reached the intersection, a delivery truck approached from my right and slowed down as it reached a stop sign. It was early enough in the day that there was absolutely no other traffic on either street; we were the only two moving objects in the scene.

The timing of this sequence could not have been choreographed more precisely. I entered the intersection just a moment before the truck got to the stop sign. This was not a four-way stop; I had the right of way. And I assumed, foolishly, that the driver saw me.

Just at the point at which I expected the truck to come to a complete stop and wait for me to pass, the driver hit the gas pedal.

The moment I realized that the driver had not seen me came just as I crossed in front of the truck. I made a noise that I have never heard before, a loud grunt that rose from my diaphragm. It was like I had been punched in the stomach. I'm not sure why, but my instinct was to stop running and put up my right hand.

The driver must have seen me as soon as he pressed the accelerator because he immediately hit the brakes and stopped about a foot from my hand.

I find the binary nature of this kind of moment perplexing. But for a second or two, that scene would have been life-changing for both me and the driver. We could have been linked forever, indelibly imprinted on each other's lives. Instead, we didn't even speak. After a fraction of a second, I turned away and continued my run and he drove off.

As I ran home, I thought briefly about how stupidly I'd acted. I had behaved on foot as though I was driving a car. I had the right of way, so I kept running into an intersection without checking first that the driver could see me. But what good would the right of way have done me if I was about to become a hood ornament?

I'd like to tell you that incident was enough to turn me into a more safety-conscious runner, but I made the same mistake again a few weeks later. This time, the driver noticed me more quickly and I was not yet in front of her, so it was less dramatic. But I realized I still hadn't learned my lesson.

And not long after, I read about a cyclist who was killed when passing in front of a bus. I didn't find out all the details right away, but it seemed to fit into a category of the easy but dangerous mistakes you can make as a runner or cyclist, mistakes I've made many times myself:

You're in the zone. When you've got music in your headphones and you're on a runner's high, you may not be sufficiently focused on the traffic around you.

You don't want to interrupt the flow of a good run or ride. Nobody likes to constantly slow down and speed up during a run or ride. I've crossed against red lights and cheated yellow lights in the name of keeping up my pace. But if you need to maintain a certain tempo, it is much safer to do it in a setting without traffic, like on a bike path.

You assume the driver can see you. I sometimes fall into the trap of thinking that because I can see the car, the driver must be able to see me. But I'm a lot smaller than the car and I'm not inside a box with obstructions in my field of vision. And when I'm running in the dark, I'm practically invisible. I should probably wear more reflective clothing.

You probably ride your bike like you drive your car. I've made the mistake of weaving in and out of traffic, but I've come to realize that I'm catching drivers off guard and that the equivalent of a minor fender-bender in my car would be a dangerous accident on my bike.

As a runner, you think of yourself as a pedestrian. But you're moving much more quickly than someone walking. Therefore it's more likely that you'll surprise a driver.

You think it's safer when there's less traffic. It's not. Drivers tend to be a lot less cautious when there's less traffic. If it had been later in the morning and there had been cars and other pedestrians on the road, my scene with the delivery truck would never have happened.

We are taught defensive driving but not defensive running. And as a runner, there's an extra incentive to be careful: if you collide with a car or truck, you'll pay a greater price than the driver.

Instead of putting the onus on drivers and foolishly exerting the right of way, I made a decision to put my safety first. I'm going to try repeating that mistake again.

iRun for Team in Training CHERYL POLLOCK, ONTARIO

Some people run for themselves, to stay in shape, to achieve personal goals, or to get away from it all and clear their minds.

Jane Spiteri was one of those runners, until she started training for a different reason.

"Running for me is a very selfish thing," says Spiteri. "It takes me away from my family, it's my time. But then I thought, it's time for me to do something for someone other than myself."

Not long after running the half-marathon at Ottawa Race Weekend, Spiteri saw an ad in iRun magazine for Team in Training, a program run by the Leukemia and Lymphoma Society of Canada. Many years ago, the charity was the first to see a fundraising opportunity in exotic marathons and other destination races. They started training runners for popular international events and covered their travel costs if they raised enough donations for the cause.

What first caught Spiteri's attention was the chance to run a race she'd always wanted to enter: the Nike Women's Half-Marathon in San Francisco.

"It started off as a destination run," she says. "I wanted to go somewhere different to run and I saw this as a way to do it."

Like most, Spiteri's family has been touched by cancer. But

she has no particular connection to leukemia. Before long, however, Spiteri was hooked on the cause and the program. She remembers something that caught her eye around the time she was researching Team in Training.

"There were four obituaries for women under the age of forty who had died of cancer that week," she says. "That was another motivating factor to do something. I'm not running for a person, I'm running for the cause."

Spiteri set out to raise her target of $5,000. At first it seemed like a daunting task, but she was astonished by the response when she asked for help.

"The generosity of people is just overwhelming sometimes," says Spiteri. "My fundraising went so much better than I thought it would and it was all because of the generosity of friends and family. People are so supportive."

Spiteri ended up raising more than $6,500. In fundraising and in running, sometimes you can surprise yourself.

"This has been a very empowering experience," she says, "to know that you can do a little bit for yourself, but you're doing a whole lot for something else."

Running for a cause has also given her a new perspective on her training.

"Running for two-and-a-half hours is hard," she says. "But you think about what people who have been afflicted by this disease go through. You think running is hard. Running is nothing compared to chemotherapy."

Team in Training supports its runners with coaching and sets up a virtual team of runners: a community in which runners can interact with others who are training for the same race. Spiteri is one of a group of eight runners from Ottawa who were planning to run either the Nike event or the Chicago Marathon in 2009. She says the coaching, and the e-mails from other team members, have helped motivate her to train and fundraise.

Before joining the team, Spiteri didn't know any of the other runners from Ottawa. But before long they were connecting by e-mail and organizing a joint fundraising event to add to their totals. They hosted a reception with a live auction and silent auction to raise more money for the cause.

Spiteri wanted to make sure as much money as possible goes to leukemia research. So, she made her own donation to the charity and chose to fly to San Francisco on points to save the program the cost of her flight.

There, after training mostly on her own for months, Spiteri was among thousands of team members at the start line.

According to organizers, as many as one-quarter of the runners in the Nike race are from Team in Training, from across North America. Each of them wears a purple team T-shirt to show their numbers and demonstrate their support for the cause.

"I can't wait for this race," said Spiteri before she left for San Francisco. "I just get shivers thinking about it. They say it's supposed to be a life-altering experience. And I can see that it's going to be."

And, even before she completed her first race as a fundraiser, she's already thinking about signing up again.

"When I started doing this, I thought, well this is going to be a one-time event. But I'm going to be wearing that purple shirt again without a doubt."

[NOTHING CAN HELP YOUR RUNNING]

iRun for the TAPER! SANDRA ROBERTS, QUEBEC

You've been training for months. You've done all the long runs, in good weather and in bad. You've crawled out of bed for an early-morning run and still been back in time to be the first person in your house to hit the shower. You've done exhaustive hill training and heart-pounding speedwork. Now, with one week to go before the big event, it's time for you to do the most important thing you can to help your race-day performance:

Nothing.

It's not that there's nothing you can do, it's that nothing is the thing to do. And if you thought the last long run before a marathon is tough, it can be just as hard not running at all. This is taper time. It's the *Seinfeld* of training weeks.

Apart from a few easy runs and some short distances at race pace, tapering is the time to dial it down. Sound easy? It's not.

After pumping myself up for weeks, I find it tough to resist the urge to run hard and often the week before a race. Especially for marathon runners, running less feels counterintuitive. You've been running long distances for weeks. If you don't run, won't your muscles lose strength? If you take it easy, will you have the energy you need on race day? Shouldn't you just get in one more long run to get your legs in perfect shape?

No. Instead, you're told that good, hard training doesn't improve your body, it actually harms it. It's the rest and recovery after training when your body improves. And if you want to be in the best possible condition on race day, you need to give your body a little R&R.

Running coaches recommend quality over quantity in the final few days. And on the final day before the race, it's really time to do absolutely nothing. Some runners like to go out for a short jog just to stretch their legs, but many coaches recommend sitting on the couch and watching movies all day. No, you're not hallucinating; your coach is actually telling you not to run.

The taper is the most important part of the training program, one coach told me. Bottom line: if you're not rested and enthusiastic at the start line, you won't run well.

The good news is that as you cut back on your volume, your legs will feel more energetic. And that will help build your confidence leading up to race day.

God knows you'll need it. Because conveniently, as you cut back on your kilometres, you'll find you have a bit of extra time to do what comes more naturally: worrying about the race. You can rest your body, but just try resting your mind.

For the first few months of training, race day seemed like a lifetime away. How many more of these long runs do I have to do, you were thinking. Now, it's hurtling toward you like Tom Cruise at a Scientology convention.

The last week before a marathon is like the last five minutes before a final exam. There is still time to worry about what could go wrong, but no time left to do anything about it. The good news is that if you don't think you're ready, it's probably not a bad sign. You don't want to be overconfident.

Besides, if it wasn't a challenge, if it wasn't something you worried about, it would hardly be worth doing.

So, I usually take all that nervous energy and invest it in obsessing about race-day details. What are you going to eat the day before? The night before? The morning of the race? How many times can you check that all your clothes are laid out and ready for race day? The only way to make sure you don't forget something is to become a control freak.

This is also the week when you'll notice every little ache and pain or tickle in your throat and think, uh-oh. This is the week when you'll stub your toe and for thirty seconds believe it's broken and your race is over. This is the week when your spouse will get a cold and you'll think about moving into a hotel.

This is also the week you'll review your race goal and strategy a few thousand times. I find myself calculating pace times on a spreadsheet on my computer. As I fall asleep, I'm thinking, do I want a negative split? By how much?

It's a week of anxiety and fighting the urge to run. But you wouldn't have it any other way. If you've done the training and have a realistic goal, there's nothing else to do but wait. Before you know it, you'll be at the start line. And then you can run forever.

[FRACTIONS]

iRun to someday win the race LINDY DUNLOP, YUKON

Is there anything more rewarding than doing something you once thought was impossible, then testing yourself and being surprised at the outcome?

I felt it the first time as a runner when I finished my first marathon. And I felt it again in May 2008 when I ran my best one.

I trained for the Mississauga Marathon with a friend who was hoping to qualify for the Boston Marathon. For him to get in, we would need to finish in less than three hours and thirty-six minutes. That wouldn't get me into Boston (I need 3:20), but it would be a few minutes better than my fastest time, so it would be a good outcome for both of us.

But three days before the race, my friend pulled out with a virus. After four months of training together, through longer and longer weekend runs and countless hill repeats and speed workouts, I was on my own. The whole experience had been intended to be a shared one. He wasn't just my training partner, he was also my ride home from the race. I actually considered not going.

But I tried to think of the last-minute twist as another challenge. So I went to Mississauga and decided to stick to our original plan: Run at a pace for a 3:30 finish and stick with it for as long as possible. Goal number one: 3:35 or better. Goal number two, if all went well: break 3:30.

In every marathon I'd done so far, I had run at one pace for thirty to thirty-five kilometres and then slowed down considerably in the final stretch. So even when I was on pace at the twenty-five kilometre point in Mississauga, I didn't know if I would sustain it.

But somehow, I managed to hang on to my pace for longer than normal. It was getting harder, and my calves were starting to cramp, but at thirty-seven kilometres, I was still on target. I was having a great race. It wasn't falling apart the way it did in other marathons.

Sometimes, I was finally discovering, it all comes together. The weather co-operates, you take on the right amount of food and water, you choose a pace that's fast enough but not too fast, and when you push on when it starts to get uncomfortable, your body doesn't quit.

I passed thirty-nine kilometres, then forty. It was getting harder and I knew that no matter how far I'd run, it could still change for the worse at anytime. But I started sensing I could finish without slowing down too much.

The course ends along a winding path by Lake Ontario, so you don't see the finish line until there's about fifty metres to go. When I saw the finish, I looked down at my watch and saw 3:29:46.

I didn't expect to have any energy left, but somehow I managed to start running faster and faster. By the time I got to the finish line, it felt like I was sprinting.

I crossed the line and stopped my watch: 3:30:01.

The numbers said I had missed my goal by one second. But something told me they were wrong. I can't explain why. Maybe I glanced down and saw the time as I crossed the line. Maybe I was just counting on the fact that I had hit the button more than a second after I crossed. I just had a feeling I had done it.

I found the spot where the printed results are posted and hovered for fifteen minutes until an employee with the timing company Sportstats appeared with a handful of paper. He posted a sheet and I scanned until I found my name: 3:29:59.1.

I made my goal and broke 3:30 by nine-tenths of a second. It was the slimmest of margins, but it was still the difference between finishing in the 3:20s and the 3:30s.

Even if I'd finished in 3:30:00.1, it would still have been my fastest and strongest marathon. And over the course of 42.2 kilometres, there are hundreds of things that could have made a difference of nine-tenths of a second, one way or the other. So you can't get too fixated on precise times.

But crossing that one extra threshold, one I never expected to cross, made it very special. And running a strong race, without slowing down, was just as satisfying. The only thing missing was my training buddy.

If there are any lessons from the experience, they are simply to remember that your training prepared you for the race, that you can keep your pace even when it starts to get uncomfortable, and that you shouldn't worry about the finish line until it's right in front of you.

I just tried to keep my pace, one kilometre at a time, until the race was over.

When I started this crazy journey, I never imagined I could run a marathon in less than three-and-a-half hours. But that's what happens when you test yourself and everything falls into place: you find out you can do something you once thought you couldn't.

[**USING YOUR HEAD**]

iRun because I've got great trails in my backyard REBECCA TAYLOR, BRITISH COLUMBIA

Dave McMahon suddenly appears on top of a huge outcropping at Camp Fortune, a giant rock that ends abruptly with a drop of four or five feet before the trail resumes below.

Only a few minutes earlier, about thirty of us had tried in succession to run up and down this rock without much success. Many of us came to almost a complete stop and then took six or seven tiny steps to lower ourselves down the steep incline.

But Dave doesn't even break stride. He bounces one step off the leeside of the rock and sprints forward on the trail, taking a sharp turn while gathering speed. By the time he stops, the rest of us are applauding.

Watching and learning from Dave, I am quickly becoming hooked on the sport of trail running. But like that rocky stretch at the top of the path, it's a leap I don't make easily.

This sport should be a natural fit for me. I like trails, I like hiking, I like running and I even like running on hills. But I hadn't done a serious trail run in almost four years.

Unfortunately, I developed an entirely unreasonable fear of injuring myself by landing awkwardly and stumbling. On my previous trail run, I turned my ankle, then started worrying about doing it again. The fear made me run cautiously and rigidly, which in turn made it more likely to happen. I turned my ankle half a dozen more times before the end of the run and gave it up, thinking I had weak ankles that couldn't stand any instability. Since then, I've stayed out of the woods.

But the opportunity to learn from a trail-running guru was too hard to resist. Dave and his wife, Lise Meloche, have been leading runners through Gatineau Park for years. They even have a video company for which Dave records spectacular trails across the country, running at high speed with a camera. In other words, while most of us struggle to negotiate a tough trail, Dave runs it while looking through the lens of a camera.

Some of Dave's recorded runs have been watched by astronauts running on the treadmill aboard the International Space Station.

Dave and Lise gave me a reintroduction to trail running that set me back on the right path. As I suspected, the problem was never in my ankles, it was in my head.

Dave taught some very useful technique for climbing, descending and turning. Trail running requires a lot more knowledge and tactics than routine jogging, and some of it is counterintuitive. You have to think on the fly and adjust your body so you're landing softly and maintaining your balance throughout your run.

But the most valuable lesson for me was how to overcome my fear of stumbling. Dave's advice was to run like you're on a track, with a normal stride, a lot of bounce in your step and a fearless attitude. As he pointed out, if you're worried about roots, rocks and branches, you'll pass over most of them in the air if you maintain a normal gait.

I imagine it's a lot like running across a series of logs floating on a river, or the rare contestant who actually manages to clear some of the crazy obstacles on the TV show *Wipeout*. If you quickly spring off every surface your foot strikes, you're a lot less likely to stumble. The more time your foot spends on the ground, the more likely it is to get you in trouble.

All of which is easier said than done. But by the time the clinic was over, I felt like I had overcome my mental block. In the space of two hours, I went from nervous to comfortable. By the time we had finished, I was ready to do it all over again.

There was still a lot to learn, but I felt like I'd crossed a mental divide much greater than the rock that Dave bounded across. I had a whole new world of running I could blend in with my existing training.

The trails offer a break from the monotony of road running and a different challenge that can help you improve overall technique. And they often provide shelter from the blazing sun and a completely different climate from a summer run on exposed city streets.

Not to mention the scenery. Canada is blessed with spectacular and well-maintained routes with a wide range of difficulty level. You could do a different run every week and not run the same route more than once a year.

You really shouldn't be a runner in this country without taking advantage of the trails. Which is why, thanks to a little more technique and a lot more confidence, I figured I would be doing this again soon.

[**WALLY AND JOHN**]

iRun because I cannot stop LAINA ANDREWS, ONTARIO

At the start line of the Ottawa Fall Colours Marathon in 2009 were two old friends with a thousand marathons between them.

Wally Herman, the ageless Ottawa endurance athlete, and John Wallace, a native of Carleton Place who now lives in Florida, both entered the scenic event in Cumberland, the eastern part of the city, where they added to their astonishing career totals.

Herman is a legendary figure in the sport, having completed 714 marathons (the same number of home runs Babe Ruth hit) at the time of his Ottawa run. At age eighty-three, he wasn't entering races as frequently as he used to. For him, that meant doing "only" nine or ten marathons a year, more than most runners do in a lifetime.

Wallace, who was sixty-five, had run 321 marathons. He happened to be in town for a wedding and family reunion, so he decided to join his friend and mentor in the race.

Herman actually joined the Fall Colours on the anniversary of his first marathon in 1975. In the 1970s and '80s, he was one of the first to start piling up a long list of races.

"The first one, I thought, I'll do one and that's it, I'll get it out of my system," he says. "But then you're hooked."

Herman started travelling North America by bus, buying ten-day Greyhound passes so he could run a marathon in one city one weekend and another the next. Along the way, he became the first person to run a marathon in all fifty U.S. states and one of the first to complete races on all seven continents, including Antarctica.

"I just enjoy getting out there," he says.

Interestingly, it took him longer to complete the shorter list of Canadian provinces and territories than the fifty U.S. states.

The only marathon in the Yukon fell on his wedding anniversary every year, so it took some time to convince his wife to let him go run it.

And then when a new territory, Nunavut, was added years later?

"I went and ran there, too," says Herman.

Over the last three-and-a-half decades, he's become friends with other multiple-marathoners, including two who have even higher totals than his.

By the time Wallace started compiling his list, Herman and others were far ahead of him. But he has the advantage in another category – Wallace is believed to be the only person in the world to run marathons in 100 different countries.

"I thought, I'm never going to catch Wally in the number of marathons he's run," says Wallace. "And trying to be the first to do anything in running is very, very difficult. So I'm going to try to run the most number of countries in the world. I finally caught Wally last year."

Herman has run in ninety-nine countries. Wallace has offered to run with him in a 100th country, but so far, Herman has declined because he's cut back on travelling.

Wallace has run marathons in every country in Europe, and completed races in exotic places like the Himalayas, on the Inca Trail in Peru and in the Sahara Desert.

"I've always had a rule," he says. "I don't go anywhere unless there's a marathon."

A former technology executive and federal civil servant, Wallace worked in high tech in the U.S., where he took up running to relieve stress. But, like Herman, he got hooked.

"It's an addiction," he says.

Wallace retired early and followed his wife when her job was transferred to Europe.

"I said, 'While you're working your butt off, I'm going to travel around Europe and run some marathons.' We were there a year and I had run thirty-one marathons in thirty-one countries."

After running in ten more countries, Wallace figured, "I must be almost done Europe. I'm going to finish Europe off. It turns out that was a brash statement. There are a lot more countries in Europe than you think there are."

Wallace is now working on completing North and Central America. He needs only Guatemala to finish that set.

"A quarter of the places I've run, I wouldn't have even considered going if there hadn't been a marathon," he says. "And then when I get there, I really enjoy the country. Because every country's got interesting things to see and typically the people are wonderful."

Like Herman, Wallace wants to keep entering marathons for as long as he can. But he has yet to heed the advice of his mentor to adjust his pace to avoid injuries as he gets older.

"I'm pretty hard on my body," he says. "Wally runs and walks in his races and takes his time. I'm just too competitive. I try to win every race, at least in my age category. And I seem to be coming up with more and more injuries. Wally keeps telling me to slow down."

The Ottawa Fall Colours event didn't add another country to

Wallace's total, but it's still had a special attraction for him.

"It's Wally's hometown," he says, "and I consider it my native hometown. So I'm there."

[**A NATIONAL PRIDE**]

iRun because of Terry Fox GRANT BOLAND, QUEBEC

Maybe it's a bit of national pride showing through, but I couldn't help feeling my blood pressure rise over what *Runner's World* magazine considered the most significant events and people in the sport from the past forty years. The oversights on the list are shocking; so is the editors' choice as the only Canadian who actually makes the cut.

Runner's World is the bible of long-distance running. It's published in the U.S., where the majority of its subscribers live, but it's read and respected by runners around the world. So when *Runner's World* celebrated its fortieth anniversary with a series of nostalgic articles about the history of the magazine and the sport, it was a significant milestone.

To mark the occasion, the editors picked the forty most notable individuals and moments from running in the past forty years. "These stunning achievements, inspiring ideas and bold exploits were revolutionary in their time," the magazine wrote, "but the true measure of their impact is their lasting legacy."

It wasn't specified, but it quickly became apparent that any lasting legacy must occur in the U.S. Of the thirty-two people *Runner's World* honoured (along with eight events), twenty-six are from the U.S. Many of them are deserving: Kathrine Switzer, who forced her way into the men-only Boston Marathon in 1967, Brian Maxwell, who invented the PowerBar, and legendary runners such as Steve Prefontaine, Bill Rodgers and Frank Shorter.

But the magazine made only a token effort to recognize how truly international the sport of running is and always has been. Norway's Grete Waitz received prominent attention, but that's only because her greatest achievement was winning the New York marathon nine times.

There was only a brief nod to the utter domination of recent marathon races by Kenyan runners. At the time of the publication, Kenyan men had won fourteen of the previous sixteen Boston marathons, six of the last nine in New York and five of the last six Chicago marathons.

This command of the podium earned Kenyan athletes a total of two short paragraphs. Whereas Americans winning a silver and a bronze in the 2004 Olympic marathon was rated as the sport's only significant event of the previous five years.

Overlooked from that same time period was Britain's Paula Radcliffe, who dramatically closed the gap between the marathon world records for women and men. She was nowhere to be found.

The same goes for Hicham El Guerrouj, the inspiring Morrocan world-record holder in the mile who pulled off a rare double gold medal in the 1,500 and 5,000 at the Athens Olympics.

Speaking of milers, there was also no mention of Britons Steve Ovett and Sebastian Coe, whose rivalry dominated middle-distance running twenty-five years ago, and who duelled for the world record in the mile, setting three new standards in ten days in August 1981.

All these great athletes were missing, but Oprah Winfrey was there. What's Oprah's "stunning achievement" or "bold exploit" that has a "lasting legacy?" Running the 1994 Marine Corps Marathon.

No question that Oprah helped spawn a new generation of runners by empowering women who thought a marathon was impossible. But is that really one of the forty most significant events of the past forty years?

Most shocking, though, was the Canadian for which *Runner's World* did save one spot in its top forty. Was it Donovan Bailey, who set a world record in the 100 metres in 1996 and then beat Michael Johnson in a 150-metre race to satisfy any doubt that he was the world's fastest man?

No. The lone significant Canadian runner from the past forty years was Ben Johnson. There was even a picture of Johnson in his Canadian uniform from the 1988 summer Olympics. Johnson, of course, is the poster boy for drugs in the sport, but it's not like he was the only one who's ever tested positive.

He's also not even close to having the greatest impact of a Canadian runner of the past forty years. Here's another idea for you, *Runner's World*. Want a Canadian on your list? How about Terry Fox?

If it's bold exploits you're after, how about running more than 5,000 kilometres in less than five months, a pace of 37.5 kilometres per day? Inspiring ideas? How about deciding to run across the second-largest country in the world to raise money for cancer research?

If it's stunning achievements you want, how about doing all of that on one leg? Dean Karnazes doesn't run that far on two legs and he was on the cover of your magazine.

Terry's no Oprah Winfrey, of course, but if you're looking for a lasting legacy, how's this: there have been Terry Fox Runs held in fifty countries around the world. So far, more than $400 million has been raised for cancer research in the name of Terry Fox.

As Terry Fox's international legacy demonstrates, the sport of running is embraced by people all over the planet. Running isn't an American invention, nor have Americans exclusively revolutionized the sport. You'd think a publication with "World" in its name would recognize that.

To its credit, *Runner's World* published a feature on Terry Fox not long after its fortieth anniversary issue. But it still baffles me that they overlooked him in the first place.

[THE CHARM OF THE SMALLER EVENT]

iRun for the scenery CRYSTAL PARTON, SASKATCHEWAN

I like big events. I like to stand in a massive wave of runners and share in the optimism and expectation of a start line, like the one at the New York City Marathon.

I like to see loud, encouraging spectators lining almost every part of the route and a big, roaring crowd at the finish.

But I've discovered small races can have their own special charm. In 2009, I ran the Green Mountain Marathon in Vermont. Haven't heard of it? I hadn't either, until a month before.

It started with a simple objective: My training partner and I set out to find a fall marathon within driving distance on a day without scheduling conflicts.

By process of elimination, the Vermont race became our best option. The prospect of running in scenic Vermont in the autumn was appealing, but the choice had more to do with logistics than anything else.

But the more we learned about the race, the better it sounded. Generally, you don't like to find the word "mountain" in the title of a marathon, but it turns out that's misleading.

The Green Mountain Marathon is run along a relatively flat course on an island in Lake Champlain where, according to the race website, you can "explore the New England of long ago" in a "land of farms, apple orchards and summer cottages."

We decided to stay in nearby Plattsburgh, New York, which is not the New England of long ago.

In fact, our accommodations at the Super 8 motel were closer to the Family Vacation of 1978, but the room rate was irresistible: $58 U.S. per night.

I think that would have paid for three hours at the hotel in Manhattan where I stayed for the marathon in 2006.

The night before the race, we ate our pre-race meal at a restaurant where it felt like we were the only people who didn't know the owner. The next morning, we set off at 7:15 to take the ferry to the island.

Unlike most running events today, the Green Mountain Marathon is just a marathon. There is no half-marathon, no 10k, no 5k, no 2k family run or 1k kids' race. And the race is almost deliberately low-tech and low-key. It started right outside a public school in a place called South Hero, Vermont (yes, there's a North Hero too; we ran through it).

The race T-shirt had no sponsor logos on it, just the name of the event and the date (and like the mountain, it was green). There wasn't a giant race expo, just a simple registration process in the school gym.

And for last-minute bathroom breaks, you joined a small lineup outside the school washroom.

There I met a very pleasant Vermont native who had run the Ottawa Marathon in May (and a less interesting man who made a point of telling both of us, apropos of nothing, without any prompting and within ten seconds of meeting us, that he had run more than 100 marathons).

At the start line, there was no big banner or balloons. No public address system either, not even a megaphone. There was just a guy standing on the roof of a car. In a normal voice, he reminded everyone who had run the race last year that there was a slight change to the course and then said, "Ready, set, go!"

More than half of the race was run on dirt roads with a spectacular view of Lake Champlain. The website was right about the atmosphere. It was like running a marathon and stepping into an episode of Newhart at the same time (I forgot to check for runners named Darryl and Darryl).

The roads weren't closed to cars, so every once in a while, a vehicle would navigate through the runners slowly and carefully.

That was only a minor inconvenience and it made it very easy for spectators to follow the runners. I saw the same people on the sidelines over and over again. They cheered, got back in their cars, drove ahead and parked, and then cheered again.

Nevertheless, the course was a bit lonely at times. There was a 5k stretch where I saw only about a dozen people, including both spectators and runners. There were times when it felt closer to an early-morning training run than a race. Still, the spectators were there when you needed them and they were especially noisy and supportive near the finish line.

There are probably only a handful of marathons that are closer to home than Green Mountain (the trip was less than three hours each way) and none with the same small-town, colonial charm. And yet until recently, I didn't even know this race existed.

After we finished the race, my friend and I drove back to the ferry. As we sailed across Lake Champlain, I set a new goal for myself. I still dream of entering big-city marathons, but I'm going to start seeking out some small ones, too.

[OVERWHELMING AND ENERGIZING]

iRun for the thrill of it JULIA REYNOLDS, CALIFORNIA

Yes, smaller races have their charm. I like the well-organized neighbourhood run, the rural half-marathon, the charity 5k with one or two hundred participants. To be honest, there aren't too many race settings that don't appeal to me.

But there's nothing like lining up at the start line of a large event – or a few hundred metres back from the start line – surrounded by thousands of other runners and a few hundred porta-potties. Here's what I love about the overwhelming, claustrophobic, empowering and energizing big-city race day experience:

• Pushing through the overcrowded expo, a room drowning in hope, anticipation, nervous energy and free samples

• Taking the official T-shirt out of the race kit even though I'm not to wear it until after I've earned it by crossing the finish line

• Watching an entire city like New York or Ottawa embrace its event and hearing "Good luck" or "Congratulations" from total strangers

• Approaching the start line and seeing the crazy number of people of all ages, colours, shapes and sizes who are wearing race bibs

• Crowding into the starting area and seeing nothing but runners in front of you and behind

• Watching the runners way ahead of you start to bounce up and down after the gun goes off

• That constant electronic hum as thousands of timing chips cross the start line

• Trying to contain the burst of excitement and not run too quickly in the first kilometre

• The rock groups, the belly dancers and the other entertainers who get up way too early in the morning to line the route and create energy for the runners

• Let's face it: it's the only time of the year where you can get away with peeing in broad daylight on the side of a major roadway

• The residents along the route who put a CD player at the end of their driveways and crank out rock tunes, or set up their own aid stations, some of them still nursing their morning coffee

• The volunteers who turn in a marathon performance of their own, staying in one place for hours as thousands run past them, holding out one cup after another and saying non-stop "Water. Water. Water."

• Seeing the elite runners glide past at speeds you couldn't match for even 100 metres

• The view of the city and the other runners you get when you're running across a bridge

• The thousands of runners who turn their race into something more than just a personal journey, by raising money for important causes

• Getting passed by someone older than you and realizing you can still get better with age

• The kids with hockey sticks steering aside the paper cups and sponges

• Watching a group of walkers patiently put down step after

step in the half-marathon or marathon and appreciating the length of their journey to the finish line

• Running past someone you haven't seen in a few years and hearing them call out your name

• Those rare spectators who stand along the less populated stretches of the route, where they really make a difference with a round of applause or an encouraging word rising above the sound of shoes hitting pavement

• Hearing the crowd noise build and knowing no matter how much it hurts, it will be over soon

• Hitting the final 500 metres, the stretch you've been imagining for three months and the noise of thousands of spectators screaming carries you to your final destination

• Looking at a total stranger running next to you at the finish and saying, or thinking, "We made it!"

• The medical personnel who appear out of nowhere to help a runner who stumbles at the finish line

• That first bite of food in the recovery area

• Two words: massage tent

• Seeing family and friends reunited with finishers, like an airport waiting area, only full of medals and foil blankets

• Standing at the finish line and watching one runner after another come in, raising their arms in triumph or bending over in pain, and how that never gets old

• Checking the Internet at the end of the day and looking up every runner you can think of

• The anticipation for the next race that starts about a minute after you cross the finish line

[**GUYS AND GADGETS**]

iRun because I am addicted to running gear MIKE ISEMAN, ONTARIO

When my friend and running buddy bought himself a GPS watch, it pretty much guaranteed I would be getting one of my own.

The GPS is the ultimate toy for the runner. I used to measure out my routes in the car or with a map and a piece of string – you know, like your grandparents did. Then I discovered Google Earth. Then, either before or after a run, I would spend ten or fifteen minutes on a computer drawing a series of little lines to map out my route. If I had a particular pace in mind, I would make mental notes about important milestones on the route, so I could make sure I was on pace at particular junctures. But that meant I could determine and adjust my pace only every few kilometres.

With a GPS, you don't have to do any of that. All the information is captured on a fairly large display on your wrist. It's a bit like something Captain Kirk would have worn, only it can't tell you how many life forms are in the vicinity.

GPS devices sometimes have difficulty connecting with satellites if you're running near tall buildings and they take readings at intervals, so you have to remember the information is more precise over a stretch of running than it is in each individual second. You shouldn't be reading the data and adjusting constantly, especially since you might end up running into a telephone pole.

Most devices also come with software that lets you download all the information into your computer to store and compare data for all your runs. If you're the kind of person who likes evaluating and analyzing your week-by-week progress, it's a handy gadget. Once my friend got his, he would disappear to his office at the end of each run and not come back until he had mined the data for an interesting fact.

"I shortened my stride for a while, and I was able to run at the same speed but with a lower heart rate," he would say. Or something to that effect.

As with any piece of technology, you can get a good deal if you buy the next-to-latest version, which is what my friend did. He showed it to me over the course of a few runs and it seemed to have all the features I needed, so I was all set to buy the same one myself.

But when I started investigating, I was told that the newer model took more frequent and accurate readings. The display was also smaller and squarer, meaning it was like an enormous wristwatch instead of a small computer attached to your arm. And it had some other new features which I can't remember now and may never use. But the point was that it was better.

There was one problem with buying the newest GPS: it cost almost $400.

But – and here's where rationalization reaches its peak – I had a chance to get a deal. I found out that if you bought a box of a particular cereal and brought it to a particular running store, you would get twenty per cent off your purchase. Twenty per cent off $400 is $80. That's a good return on a $4 investment, whether I eat the cereal or not. If I do this enough times I could retire at fifty-five.

When I began to share my plan to acquire the new, discounted GPS with my friend, I had barely started talking before he said, "Is this going to end with you saying you're getting a newer device for about what I paid for mine?" We know each other fairly well.

The look on his face told me in an instant what was about to happen. John would have to sell his outdated device and buy a newer one, after making a similar cereal-related investment. So last week, we marched into the store together, each with our cereal coupon. In fact, I brought the whole box. We now have matching devices. This is how it is with boys and their toys.

[SHOELESS RUNNING]

iRun barefoot GAIL OBORNE, MANITOBA

Imagine throwing on your T-shirt and shorts, strapping a watch to your wrist, and heading out the door for a 10k run, leaving your running shoes in the front-hall closet.

OK, maybe winter in Canada is not the time to try it. But barefoot running is taking off.

"There are definitely more people doing it," says Ryan Grant, an expert on feet and footwear. Grant, a runner, triathlete and co-owner of Ottawa's Solefit Orthotics, says, "At least half the people we see ask about it. People are trying to see how they can simplify what they're doing. It's not a fad."

The movement is driven in part by the popularity of a recently published book. In *Born to Run*, author Christopher McDougall tries to find out why he, like many other runners, was often injured.

"I was always getting hurt," says McDougall. "I was told by top sports medicine doctors for years that running is bad for you. The impact is bad for the body, that it's going to destroy your knees."

McDougall ends up finding answers in a remote part of Mexico where he discovers a tribe that runs barefoot.

"I just couldn't resolve one key question: If these guys can be running hundreds of miles when they're seventy, eighty years old, what are they doing that I'm not doing?

"Either they are some kind of weird mutant tribe of genetic super people and therefore there is nothing we can learn from them. Or they are the same as we are and they're just doing something differently. It turns out they are exactly the same genetically as we are."

McDougall's controversial theory is that before shoe companies introduced cushioned footwear for runners, there were fewer injuries. Is the extra padding giving us protection or is it changing our biomechanics and leading to more problems?

Grant says it's true there are more injuries today. But there are also a lot more runners. "There are so many more people doing it," he says. "Thirty years ago, the only people doing the marathon were the people who were really predisposed to running. Now, people are getting off the couch and running a marathon. And the more people who are running, the more people are running with the wrong footwear."

McDougall says what he learned from the Tarahumara Indians is partly about attitude and partly biomechanics. He says to run better, you have to run more like a child. "They run with elation and joyfulness. A guy like (marathon champion) Paul Tergat has the same kind of stride as your average five-year-old. What children do instinctively, that's what Kenyans do."

And McDougall says if you're wearing a cushioned shoe, you're more likely to land on your heel than your mid-foot. Other books, like Chi Running, have argued that you need a different running stance, one that has you leaning forward and landing mid-foot, to perform better and avoid injury. McDougall takes it a step further by saying that by removing your shoes, you're more likely to do that than if you're wearing shoes.

"It was like night and day. It literally gave me back the use of my legs. I was not able to run. Now, I can do twenty miles and not even blink."

Grant says while there is merit to what McDougall argues, and the principles of techniques like Chi Running, it's not as simple as saying that shoes are bad.

"I do think that the principles have a lot of practical use," he says. "The problem with a lot of those theories is that you take someone who's not predisposed to it – someone who doesn't have the flexibility or the strength – and throw them out there barefoot, they're going to have problems."

Grant says if you put in the work to improve your flexibility and strength – that means doing yoga, getting massage therapy and adding strength training to your routine – you can eventually make the adjustment to running barefoot.

"The barefoot running theory is fantastic," he says. "There is value to simplifying. But it's not just a matter of going out and running differently. All the other principles have to be in place to support it."

Grant says if you are interested in running barefoot or similar techniques like Chi Running, you should sign up for a clinic and approach it slowly. But don't throw away your shoes just yet.

"In the grand scheme of things, shoes probably are a bit of a Band-Aid. But for most of us who have nine-to-five jobs and a life outside of running, to be able to put on a pair of motion-control shoes keeps us injury-free."

And, in winter in Canada, they also keep our feet warm.

[FINDING MORE AT THE FINISH]

iRun because there's a lot more race left in me JOHN LAFOREST, ALBERTA

Nine-and-a-half kilometres into a 10k race in 2008, I felt like I was at the breaking point. I wasn't sure if I would finish the race. But once I saw the finish line, the fatigue seemed to disappear and I started running much faster.

In a marathon the previous May, I was fighting increasing fatigue through the final five kilometres. With every step, I felt like I was getting closer and closer to the precipice. But with 200 metres to go and a personal-best time within my grasp, all of a sudden I was sprinting.

Why is it that you can go from the brink of physical exhaustion, wondering whether you can even take another step, to having a surge of energy and a higher level of performance?

It's because physical fatigue isn't entirely physical. And that's not just a cliché like mind over matter. The prevailing scientific theory is that when you feel like your muscles are at the breaking point, they really aren't. It's just your brain telling you to stop.

The idea that your brain has a lot to do with physical performance isn't new. There has always been a sense that mental toughness can override physical obstacles or that poor physical performance can be caused by mental limitations. Or, as Arnold Schwarzenegger once said, "the mind always poops out before the body."

That's not the most articulate or scientific explanation. But there's an increasing amount of research that proves he may be right. A few years ago, scientists developed what is known as the "central governor theory." It has nothing to do with the former governor of California, apart from the fact that it supports his "poop-out" theory.

The thinking used to be that your brain simply passed on a message from your muscles at the point of exhaustion. Either your muscle fibres were spent or they were overcome by toxins like lactic acid, putting a physical limit on your performance.

But researchers studied muscle fibre and found that when athletes feel totally fatigued, they actually still have reserves to draw on. The brain doesn't let your muscles go to the brink because it's worried about the risk of damage to your body. So it creates the sensations that you understand to be fatigue.

It's a bit like your car turning on a warning signal when you're low on fuel rather than when you run out of gas completely. Only in the case of your body, the warning signal hurts.

The researchers who developed this theory figure that the brain forms an idea of what a safe level of exertion is, based on the current state of your body and past experiences with strenuous exercise. That's why they think interval training is valuable: it teaches your brain that you can safely exert at a higher level.

And that's not the only way that your brain can artificially limit your performance. Other research suggests that being mentally tired before you exercise or race can make you feel physically exhausted even sooner, even though there's no difference in the performance of your muscles.

According to a study to be published in the *Journal of Applied*

Physiology, athletes who were given a mentally tiring task before exercise reached exhaustion sooner than when they were mentally rested before their workout.

Scientists had a group of athletes perform a mentally fatiguing task and then ride stationary bikes to the point of physical exhaustion. Then the same group rode the stationary bike when they were mentally rested. When they were mentally tired, they reached the point of physical exhaustion fifteen per cent faster. But here's the interesting part: scientists were measuring indicators of their muscle performance. And there was no difference in results at the same point in each workout. The riders just felt exhausted and quit earlier when they were mentally exhausted.

The researchers figure there could be two explanations. Either mental fatigue lowers your brain's resistance to quitting, or mental fatigue affects the level of a chemical in your brain called dopamine, that plays a role in motivation and effort.

Either way, the research confirms it's your brain that generally tells you to stop, not your muscles. And it helps to explain why a training run at the end of a long day at work may seem more exhausting than one first thing in the morning.

It would be a stretch to say it's all in your head. There are physical limitations to performance and it's risky to push too hard when your body is telling you to stop. But if you recognize that even though your brain is trying to look after your overall best interests, it can be an obstacle to peak performance, you may be able to overcome the signals of exhaustion and hang on for a strong result.

In other words, don't let your mind poop out before your body.

$$\left[\ \textbf{A SOLDIER'S STORY}\ \right]$$

iRun because some soldiers can't anymore D. KENNEDY, NOVA SCOTIA

After losing both of his legs while on duty in Afghanistan, Master Cpl. Jody Mitic wasn't trying to get on with his life. He was trying to get back to the battlefront. And one step on that unlikely journey was doing his first half-marathon in the 2009 Army Run.

For civilians, the Army Run is a unique race experience in which you run side-by-side with Canada's military. For soldiers, it's about esprit de corps. And for the few dozen wounded soldiers who walk, run and roll in the Army Run, it's about proving they can still be active despite their injuries.

But for Mitic, it was about showing himself and others that he can return to serving his country in one of the most dangerous regions of the world.

"My ultimate goal is, I plan to redeploy to Afghanistan," said Mitic before the race. "For the army to allow that to happen, I have to prove to them that I can do it. And to myself, too.

"So part of doing the Army Run is to show myself and to show my colleagues that I can handle the rigours of redeploying to Afghanistan. That's the ultimate reason for anything that I've been doing for the last year and a half."

In January 2007, about a week after his thirtieth birthday, Mitic was on patrol in Afghanistan when he stepped on a landmine. He lost both his legs below the knee.

"I was a sniper-team leader," he says. "We were operating in three-man teams for this tour. I was the last man in line during the patrol. I detonated a device that took one leg and then they amputated the other one surgically after."

After a long rehabilitation process, Mitic started running again on prosthetic legs. But it was a long learning process.

"In the military, running is a mainstay of our fitness routine," he says. "It's a simple thing to do every day to keep in shape. After I was wounded and learned how to walk again, running just seemed like a natural first step in regaining my fitness level.

"It was a little rough at first. It's not like you slap them on and it's just like having your old feet."

But Mitic managed to complete a 5k charity run in March 2008, raising $40,000 for the hospital where he had been treated.

"It hurt a lot," he says. "It took me almost an hour to finish. I did it, but it wasn't pretty."

Mitic worked as an outreach co-ordinator for Soldier On, a program that helps injured soldiers maintain their fitness and develop a healthy lifestyle. Soldier On is one of the recipients of the proceeds of the Army Run.

He planned to do the 5k at the inaugural Army Run in September 2008, but his daughter was born just days before the race. So he ran the charity run again the following March, raising even more money, and then devised a more ambitious plan. He decided he would run a marathon. The half-marathon in the Army Run would be a step toward that goal.

Along the way, he learned how to overcome the challenges of running on prosthetic legs. When he had completed his longest run to date on his new legs, sixteen kilometres, he noticed he had come to appreciate running more than he did before he was injured.

"I am starting to enjoy it," he says. "Running wasn't something I enjoyed beyond the 10k mark because it started to hurt. Now, I'm getting to the point where I've found a groove and it's starting to become an obvious choice for me to maintain my fitness for the rest of my life. The fitter you are as amputee, the better your quality of life."

It helps that he gets a lot of support. Mitic says when he trains along the Rideau Canal, other runners react enthusiastically when they cross paths with him.

"Sunday mornings, we run along the canal and it's nothing but cheers and thumbs-up and waves and lots of 'Awesome' as you run by," he says. "If that's the way it's going to be on the Army Run, probably times 100, it really helps your motivation to finish."

And if he can run a half-marathon and then a marathon, Mitic figures he can go back to Afghanistan.

"I've been in the military since I was seventeen," he says. "It's what I do, and I'm hoping to keep doing it. And if I can't keep doing it, I need to exhaust all possible avenues for myself before I decide to look for other employment.

"It's all I've done my whole adult life. And I love it."

[FATHERS AND SONS]

iRun to defy doubts MEGHAN O'KEEFE, ONTARIO

When I was a kid, my dad and I had a routine after Sunday mass. Once we walked through the doors of the church, we would race to the car. He would take the early lead and then – somehow – I would overtake him in the final few steps and touch the car a fraction of a second before him.

That's one of the things that fathers are good at: running with their kids. Outside of playgrounds and church parking lots, there are countless fathers who push their kids in joggers while on training runs.

Still, there's one dad who has probably run with his kid more than any other father in the world.

In January 1962, Rick Hoyt was born with severe brain damage. The doctors didn't give his parents much hope.

"The doctor said, 'Forget Rick,'" Dick Hoyt, Rick's father, once said in an interview. "'Put him away. Put him in an institution. He's going to be nothing but a vegetable for the rest of his life.'

"We cried a little bit. We talked and we said, 'No, we're not going to put Rick away. We're going to bring Rick home and bring him up like any other child.'"

That wasn't the first time the Hoyts chose to believe in their son despite what doctors told them. They taught him the alphabet, tried to get him into public school, but no one believed he could communicate.

"We knew Rick was smart," Dick said. "We could tell by looking in his eyes."

Finally, a team of researchers from Tufts University confirmed what the Massachusetts-based family had always believed: Rick understood. The engineers built Rick an interactive computer that would allow him to type using slight movements of his head.

At age ten, the kid who was supposed to spend his life in a vegetative state proceeded to type his first words: "Go Bruins." Three years later, Rick was going to school. He has since graduated from university and has a job and his own apartment.

In 1977, Rick heard about a charity run for a paralyzed athlete. He told his father he wanted to enter it. Dick wasn't a runner, but he pushed Rick through the five-kilometre run, finishing second last.

"Next-to-last," Dick said, "but not last."

After the race, Rick typed the message that would change both their lives.

"When we got home that night," Dick said, "Rick wrote on his computer, 'Dad when we're running, it feels like my disability disappears.'"

That was all Dick needed to hear. They kept running, and running.

After a few years of running, they started doing triathlons. Dick hadn't been on a bike since he was a child, and he had to learn how to swim, but that's what a father does when it makes his disabled son feel alive. They completed their first triathlon on Father's Day in 1985.

More than two decades later, Dick and Rick Hoyt had completed more than 900 events. They've run the Boston Marathon 25 times. They've completed forty other marathons and more than 200 triathlons. They've done six Ironman events: Dick pulling Rick for 3.9 kilometres in a boat tied to his waist, Rick sitting in a special seat on the front of Dick's bike for 180 kilometres, Dick pushing Rick in a wheelchair for a 42k run.

In the process, they have become celebrities in the triathlon world, rivaling the status of the world champions. Dick has run a 2:40 marathon, something ninety-nine of 100 runners couldn't do alone, let alone while pushing a man in a wheelchair. At sixty-five, he ran with Rick to a 3:43 finish in Boston last year.

What would his time have been if he ran by himself? We'll never know because he never tried.

"There's just something that gets into me when I'm out there competing with Rick that I can't explain and we're able to go faster," Dick said. "It's just an unbelievable feeling."

Besides, he thinks of Rick as the athlete.

"Rick is my motivator," Dick said. "He inspires me. To me, he's the one out there competing and I'm just loaning him my arms and my legs so that he can compete."

They've raised a lot of money for charity and inspired a lot of other athletes.

If these guys can do an Ironman, after all, surely you can complete the race for which you've been training.

"Our message is, 'Yes, you can,'" Dick said. "You can do anything you want to do as long as you make up your mind you can do it."

What they have done for others, though, is only a sidebar to the story. At the heart of it all is just what a father does for his son, making him feel alive, taking away his disability as often as he can.

"I may be disabled, but I live a very fulfilling life," Rick has said.

Try to get through the YouTube video of Dick and Rick crossing the finish line, Rick's arms waving enthusiastically, without choking up.

There is, however, one thing Rick would do if only he was able.

"The first thing he'd do," Dick said, "is have me sit down in his wheelchair and push me."

[A GOOFY EXCUSE TO RUN]

iRun for the medals and T-shirts JOHN BLACK, ONTARIO

Does this prove I love running?

Imagine you're on a relaxing family vacation by the beach in Sarasota, Florida, as I was in January 2010. Would you:

- Drive two hours to Orlando to sleep on the couch in your friend's Disney hotel room?
- Rise at 3:30 the next morning, dress in the dark and board a monorail to the Epcot Centre?
- Brave two-degree weather and ice pellets while waiting ninety minutes at the start line?
- Wear a grey hoodie and red flannel pyjama bottoms with white snowflakes that you bought at Target two days earlier because you needed some throwaway clothing at the start?
- Run a race that started at 5:40 in the morning, in the aforementioned two degrees and ice pellets scenario?
- Drive two hours back to Sarasota to resume your family vacation?

I did. That's what happens when you are on vacation and there is a race in the vicinity. You feel like you have to do it.

So we got to the start line at 4:15 and huddled with others in a tent that was supposed to be a concession area but ended up being shelter for as many runners as could comfortably fit, plus a few dozen more.

At 5:25, fifteen minutes before the start of Wave 1, we figured it was a comfortable time to find Corral A and wait for the race. We walked out of the tent and immediately heard an announcement saying it would take twenty minutes to reach the start line. Oops.

We started walking briskly toward the start. A few minutes later we heard the national anthem and not long after that, as Corral G came into view, we heard the start of the race.

The benefit of chip timing is you can start anytime up until they remove the timing devices from the start line and not really lose any time. I know someone who slept in and started the Ottawa Marathon ten minutes late but still qualified for Boston. Of course, he had to dodge a few dozen walkers to do it.

Nevertheless, we wanted to get going before the next wave. So we ran the last few hundred metres to the corral, discarding our extra layers along the way, and crossed the start line with the last few runners from A.

Over the next 3k we passed a lot of runners who would have been behind us if we hadn't been so late. We ran on the grass and on medians to get around congestion. The biggest surprise about the Disney race was that it was so dark. I guess they run the races super-early to minimize conflicts with theme-park hours and to avoid heat (not an issue that year), but the result is that instead of running in the Florida sunshine (not an issue that year), you're running on pitch-black roads between theme parks, then briefly darting through Magic Kingdom and turning back toward Epcot.

Even so, the weather wasn't a factor. It was cold and rainy but there was only one stretch, at about 17 kilometres, where I felt the wind head on. Otherwise, from my Canadian perspective anyway, the conditions were not tough.

Our goal was to get in under 1:40 so my friend Bob would qualify for New York. He was running strong and at about thirteen kilometres, I told him to go ahead if I fell behind. At that point, I was having some stomach issues and if you had asked me my chances of making my goal, I would have said five per cent. We stayed together until about fifteen-kilometre mark and then Bob started inching a little bit ahead.

I was a bit discouraged, but I started to focus on getting through each subsequent mile without losing my pace. I got to Mile 10 and then Mile 11 and I started to feel better, at least enough that it seemed possible to hang on and hit my goal.

At the final turn around the Christmas tree in Epcot, I shouted to Bob and followed him in about forty seconds later. He had a great race and finished in 1:39:11, I came in at 1:39:53.

Considering how I felt earlier, I was pretty happy with that, almost as happy as I was to receive a foil blanket to warm me for the walk back to the Monorail.

The race started so early that by 8:30 I was back at Disney's Polynesian Resort, showered and enjoying an all-you-can-eat buffet that included Mickey Mouse pancakes, wearing a Donald Duck medal and having my picture taken with Mickey.

And as for the stomach issues, I thought it might have been something I ate. But a few days later, back home in Canada, I went to the hospital with severe abdominal pain and had my appendix removed.

[RUNNING A LONG WAY FROM HOME]

iRun because being in the CF means being fit and deployable HARRY LEARNING, BRITISH COLUMBIA

Maj. Guy Leclerc wanted to participate in the 2008 Army Run in Ottawa, but he was out of the country on a training exercise.

In 2009, he was even farther away. Leclerc was serving in Afghanistan, so he would miss the run again.

So Leclerc decided to organize an Army Run of his own. Two weeks before the event in Canada, he and about 400 other members of the Canadian Forces ran around Kandahar Airfield in an event meant to mirror the one back home.

"I know there are many people like me who regret a little bit that we were not able to run the race last year," says Leclerc. "And this year again, we're not able to do it because we're here in Afghanistan. So that's where the idea came from."

The two events are separated by two weeks and 10,000 kilometres. The setting couldn't be more different.

And there will be few, if any, civilians running in Afghanistan. But when the soldiers left the start line in Kandahar, Leclerc was thinking of the thousands of civilian and military athletes who would be running two weeks later.

Probably the biggest appeal of the Army Run is that it gives civilians and Canadian soldiers the chance to run side-by-side in the same event. In the first edition, more than 7,000 runners participated in what became the most talked-about new race in Canada.

"I think it ended up being a day of coming out and supporting your troops," says Lt.-Gen. Andrew Leslie, the chief of the land staff of the Canadian Forces, who ran the 5k that year. "I was very proud of Canadians who chose to participate alongside their soldiers."

With the parallel race in Afghanistan, that connection between Canadians and their troops was extended across an ocean.

"I think it's a fantastic way to connect Canadians with their soldiers," says Maj. Chris Horeczy, the race director of the Army Run for its first two years, "to have that link right into the theatre of operations."

Instead of running along the Rideau Canal, the participants will do laps of the airfield. While runners in Ottawa might see trees and grass and stately homes, the soldiers in Kandahar will run across a bleak, dry setting far removed from civilization.

And while in Ottawa, it might be 15C on race day, in Afghanistan it will be at least twice as hot. That's why the race will start early in the day. In Afghanistan, unlike Ottawa, it is the heat and not the humidity.

"Five o'clock in the morning," says Leclerc, "so we can avoid the dust and the heat. Because right now during the day it's around forty-five and fifty degrees. It's pretty warm here."

"It's a bit of a different environment," says Horeczy. "Not quite the shade we would enjoy in Ottawa."

Another big difference is that while local runners might relax and enjoy the day after a good race, for many of the soldiers in Kandahar, the event will be a short interruption in their duties.

"A lot of them are going to go back to work that same day," says

Horeczy.

Yet despite all the differences, the two races have one common purpose: to bring the soldiers abroad closer to home and to bring Canadian civilians and soldiers closer together.

To make the connection even stronger, Horeczy brought photos and videos of the Afghanistan run home to Canada to be shown at the race expo.

"We thought it would be a tremendous way to introduce Canadians to what we're doing in Afghanistan," he says.

Horeczy figured the video helped to link two groups of Canadian runners: those at home who live in freedom with those in Afghanistan who are fighting on behalf of it.

The race in Kandahar filled up quickly. Leslie estimates that ninety-five per cent of the Canadian personnel in Afghanistan are runners, either to stay in shape for the rigours of their work or because they love the sport. On his last tour, he remembers seeing runners starting their training laps of the airfield at 4 a.m. to avoid the heat.

"Even then," he says, "it's stinking hot. But they were still out there running."

The race was organized by Canadians, but it didn't just feature Canadian military personnel. It was also open to troops from Canada's NATO allies.

"This way we meet some friends," says Leclerc. "It's the way we do it here in Afghanistan. We miss our families the same as everyone else."

Leclerc is an avid runner who has completed several marathons in Canada, including Ottawa. Though he was glad to do the new event in Afghanistan, he still dreams of one day joining the Army Run in Ottawa.

"I would like to do the one in Ottawa," he says, "but unfortunately I missed the first two editions."

Just one more reason to hope for a Canadian soldier's safe return.

[CALL HER LUCKY]

iRun because it helps me see things more clearly JENNIFER PITTS, ONTARIO

What would you consider lucky?

Would you think it's being born with no vision in one eye and only ten degrees in the other, meaning your only view of the world was like closing one eye and looking through a straw with the other?

And if that was all you could see, would you become a fitness buff? Would you climb the stairs of the CN Tower to raise money? Would you run a half-marathon?

Shelley Morris would.

Morris is just about the most enthusiastically positive person you could imagine. Her voice comes down a phone line and reaches right for your heart.

"I'm very lucky in that I was born blind, so I know nothing else," she says. "I've never had to get used to anything else. This is the way it's been all my life.

"I only see a tiny space," she says of the tunnel vision in one eye. "But you know, I've had that tiny space all my life and it's served me very well."

If you were just listening to the tone of Morris's voice, you'd swear she was describing an all-expenses-paid trip to Hawaii, not a disability she's had since birth.

Morris hasn't allowed her condition to limit her life. She's stayed active by doing aerobics and spinning. And in the 1990s, she started entering the CN Tower Climb, in which participants climb to the top of the Toronto landmark to raise money for charity. She's since done it fifteen times. Her personal best for the 144 floors, or 1,776 steps, is just over eighteen minutes.

Even though her father and sister are both long-distance runners, Morris never expected to take up the sport herself.

But in 2008, everything changed. Morris was waiting at the finish line for her sister, Colleen, and a friend as they ran the 5k at Ottawa Race Weekend.

"I was just sitting there in the park waiting for them to come back and I think I caught the vibe at that time," she says. "There was music playing. They were playing Bruce Springsteen's *Born to Run*. People were cheering. Something kind of happened that day.

"I thought to myself, this is fun. Why am I sitting here on the sidelines? I want to get involved in this. If you can climb the CN Tower, you can run a 5k."

She started training on quiet streets and paths, using her sister as a guide. The two ran side by side and Colleen gave her verbal instructions for turns and obstacles.

Gradually, she became more comfortable with running and together, the sisters have completed the Run for the Cure, the Resolution Run and the 5k at Ottawa Race Weekend.

In each race, while she can barely see anything, she still experiences it fully.

"It is amazing," she says. "The sound is all around you. It's panoramic. I can hear people's feet as I'm running. They're all around me. I'm right in the middle of it. I can hear people cheering from the sides and when they're standing up on bridges,

I can hear them up there. You'll run in and out of music, and for me, music is very inspiring. You can feel the sun on your face, and sometimes the wind on your face. It's a lot of atmosphere. Just because I don't see, I don't miss out on anything. I feel everything."

Morris says she would like to run a 10k one day. In the meantime, she hopes other people will see that if she can run, they can run.

"My message would be to inspire anybody, blind or sighted, who once thought, 'I can't run.' If somebody asked me two years ago whether I'd be running a 5k, even though all around me in my family I'm surrounded by runners, I would have said, 'No, you're crazy, I can't run, no way.'

"I just had to make that decision and look at me now. Everybody can do it."

While she inspires other runners, Morris says she herself is motivated by the military personnel and injured soldiers she was preparing to race with in the Army Run.

"I'm going to be running amongst a lot of heroes," she says.

She was one of them. Shelley Morris may think she's lucky, but so is anyone who hears her story.

$$\left[\text{ 42.2 YEARS } \right]$$

iRun for myself and others JESSICA PARSONS, QUEBEC

Sometime around my forty-second birthday, while I was on a run, it crossed my mind. Forty-two is a magic number for marathon runners, at least those of us who think in kilometres. Why not do a special marathon when I'm forty-two years old?

Then, still running, I thought of a way to take it one step – or at least one decimal point – further. I know one or two people who ran fifty kilometres on their fiftieth birthday. But fifty is a long way off and an even longer way to go. I didn't want to wait that long or run that far. So, I figured why not run 42.2k on the day I'm exactly 42.2 years old?

As I later told one person, I'm only going to be 42.2 once in my life. Why not run a marathon that day?

(I think I got a blank stare in return. Life is full of milestones, but how many people actually take note of the day they are exactly 42.2 years old?)

The math was easy. Twenty per cent of 365 is seventy-three days. Add that to my birthday and you get September 25, which, as luck would have it, fell on a Saturday. Perfect timing.

The training wasn't a big adjustment. I was already planning to run the New York City Marathon in November, so it was just a matter of accelerating the schedule.

I put out an invitation for people to join me on the run and to donate to a worthy cause: the Leukemia & Lymphoma Society of Canada. Along with motivating runners across Canada to raise money for cancer research, they've been big supporters of iRun, so it was a natural choice.

With the help of a friend, I mapped out a course along Ottawa's Rideau Canal. The plan was to run 1.1k, turn around and run back to the start, then run four out-and-back loops of ten kilometres. Presto: a marathon course covering only five kilometres.

A few people asked me whether I was worried about running so far on my own, without the other runners and crowds of an organized marathon. But the support I had before and during the run felt like ten New York City marathons.

The media got interested and told my quirky story. A few people got confused and thought it was my actual birthday, or that I was turning forty. But who cares, as long as they were talking about it?

Donations poured in. So did thoughtful words of encouragement and genuine support. I got cash and kind messages from friends and family, and from people I've never met before.

On race day, a few friends joined me at the start line. Others joined in for 5k or 10k along the way. I thought I was running pretty fast, but one friend kept up with me while pushing his two-year-old in a stroller. There was something special about the fact that people came out to run with me, just to support the crazy run I had decided to do.

It wasn't my fastest marathon but it was one of the most enjoyable. Among other things, I broke the tape at the finish line, something I'll probably never do in another race in my life.

I like numbers and milestones and I'm glad I'll always be able to say I ran my tenth marathon on the day I was exactly 42.2 years old. But here's the best statistic of all: Thanks to the generosity of friends and iRun readers, in a matter of a few weeks, we raised more than $6,500 for the Leukemia & Lymphoma Society.

[FOOTSTEPS AND FREEDOM]

iRun because I alone control how fast I can be ERIN MCDOUGALL, ONTARIO

I didn't even wear a watch. That's how serious I was about running a comfortable pace rather than racing to a fast time.

In October 2010, I ran the 9 Run Run half-marathon, a new event organized by Ottawa's police, fire and paramedic services. It was supposed to be a training run that just happened to be during a race. It ended up being my fastest half-marathon ever.

I had just run a marathon four weeks earlier and was running another two weeks later, so my plan was to run about twenty-three kilometres that weekend. Why not enter the half-marathon, run it at a training pace and tack on another two kilometres at the end?

But you know what happens at the start of a race. You get tempted to run fast.

About a kilometre into the race, my buddy Bob said "How fast do you want to go? Five minutes per kilometre?"

"Sure," I said. "Or I'm happy to try to go a bit faster and get in around 1:40 or 1:42."

"Oh," said Bob. I don't think he was expecting that.

To set the stage for you, my fastest half marathon was in 2006, when I ran 1:39:17 in another race that was supposed to be a training run just a few weeks before a marathon.

But on this day, even when I suggested we push a bit harder

than a training run, I didn't think I would end up setting a new personal best.

Bob and I maintained a strong pace together until about eleven or twelve kilometres. I know this because unlike me, Bob was wearing a watch. When he told me our pace per kilometre, I thought it translated to a finish time of around 1:42, but it turns out I was wrong. We were actually on pace for just over 1:40.

Then he suggested I go ahead if I could. And for whatever reason, I felt great. So I did pick up the pace a little and left him a few metres behind. And that's the last time until the finish line I knew how fast I was running.

The course was flat with very few turns, so it was ideal for running fast. It was also a perfect day, sunny and cool with very little wind.

About a kilometre after we split up, I heard footsteps behind me. I decided I would press a bit harder to try to hold off being passed for as long as possible. Whoever it was caught up to me and fell right in behind me, about a foot behind my shoulder. I expected him to pass me, but he just stayed there, following me step by step.

We started passing runners who had once seemed far ahead of me. For the next six kilometres, my new running partner stayed right on my tail.

With about three kilometres to go, he finally moved over so he was running next to me. "I hope you don't mind," he said, "but you're running at a good pace for me."

"Mind?" I said. "You're helping me go faster."

At this point, he sped up and left me behind. But I still felt pretty strong, so I maintained my pace and kept passing people. That's how you want to feel in the final few kilometres of a race, but it doesn't always work out that way.

With two kilometres to go, I figured I could hang on to my pace and possibly break 1:40. Remember, I had miscalculated my pace earlier in the race before I sped up.

The course turned a few hundred metres before the end and when the finish line came into view, I tried to push harder and catch up to the runner in front of me. I normally have a good finishing kick but this time it seemed harder to find another gear. Turns out that's because I was already running faster than I thought I was.

When the clock at the finish line came into view, I was hoping it wouldn't show that 1:40 had already passed. So I was surprised to see that it said 1:38. I suddenly realized I was on pace for a personal best. I ran as fast as I could and finished in 1:38:26, almost a minute better than my previous fastest time.

I was a bit shocked to find out how fast I'd been running. It was probably good that I wasn't wearing a watch, because I might have worried about whether I could sustain that pace. Instead, I ran based on how I felt and it worked out for the best. The course and the weather helped, too.

I probably shouldn't have run so fast in what was supposed to be a training run two weeks before a marathon. But if setting a new personal record in the half-marathon meant that I wasn't in ideal condition for the marathon, that was a trade I was willing to make.

[A NEW YORK DILEMMA]

iRun to stay with my friends for the long haul MIKE MALYK, MANITOBA

There are two ways to run the New York City Marathon: as a race or as a tourist attraction.

I guess there are actually a million other ways, like running in full New York City firefighter gear, or dressed as the Statue of Liberty, but I wasn't considering any of those as I prepared for the 2010 race.

In the weeks leading up to the first weekend in November, though, I was divided between those first two options. I always had it in my mind that I would run at a more leisurely pace rather than aim for a fast time. My previous experience in New York told me that racing through a crowd of almost 40,000 runners wasn't easy. And I was supposed to be running with my friend; we had trained together for New York for the past four months.

But only two weeks before the 2010 event, I set a new personal best in the half-marathon, so running fast was becoming a temptation. You don't get many chances to do a fast marathon, so if you think you're in good shape, you feel the urge to go for it.

New York, however, isn't ideal for a blistering pace. There are several significant bridges, meaning you spend a lot of time running uphill. And you have to get up in the middle of the night and get to the start line early, where you sit on the grass and kill time until the gun goes off. Unless you can sit in a yoga pose comfortably for four hours, you're legs aren't going to be in ideal shape at the start.

Still, a lot of friends and other runners were suggesting I should aim for a fast time. Right up until race morning, I wasn't sure what approach I would take.

With something as big as a marathon, your prime motivation is often the fear of regret. After the race, what would I lament more: not running with my friend and soaking up the New York experience together, or not putting in a fast time?

In the end, the answer was easy. Bob and I had trained together and this was going to be his first time running New York. Even though we always give each other a free pass to go ahead if one of us is having a better day than the other, we'd always imagined doing this race together. Plus, for all the times we'd started a marathon together, we'd never crossed the finish line side-by-side.

How could I go wrong with that as my goal? How could I regret running 42.2k through the streets of New York with my best friend?

The race was everything I remembered and everything he expected. But it wasn't all fun. On the Verrazano-Narrows Bridge, I felt a splash of liquid hit me and thought someone had spilled their water while taking a drink. A few seconds later, I looked down and saw a brown substance with the consistency of oatmeal on my shirt and shorts. The race wasn't even 10 minutes old and someone had already puked on me.

By the twenty-five kilometre mark, it became clear that I wasn't likely to have produced a fast time anyway. Maybe I was still recovering from my half-marathon or maybe it just wasn't my day, but my legs didn't feel strong. With about 10k to go, I started falling behind but Bob encouraged me to catch up and stay with him. With five kilometres to go, it was me encouraging Bob as he started flagging.

I remember saying, "We're not going to stop." We were slowing down and both of us were experiencing fatigue and nausea, but so far we had run the entire race without stopping. I figured if we started walking now, we'd be doing it a lot in the final few kilometres.

Despite the roaring crowds, the last kilometre was a struggle until the finish line was in sight. Bob said, "I'm going to raise your hand at the finish." We crossed together with our arms held high and celebrated.

It wasn't a perfect race and I still had remnants of someone's breakfast on my shorts. I'll never understand why my energy level varies from race to race and why no matter how consistently I train, some race days I can go faster than others.

But in New York in November 2010, I knew one thing: I made the right decision.

$$\left[\text{ RUNNING THE SAHARA } \right]$$

iRun for fun in the hot, hot sun CATHERINE DALE, MANITOBA

It's impossible for mere mortals like us to know what it's like to run for 111 straight days across one of the world's most desolate places. But if you want at least a slightly better idea of what's involved, get yourself a copy of the movie *Running the Sahara*.

By now, you've heard the story of how three ultramarathoners – including Ray Zahab of Canada – ran 7,000 kilometres from one side of the Sahara Desert to the other. Their epic journey in 2006 and 2007 was covered internationally; when it was over, the three were guests on the *Tonight Show* with Jay Leno.

But unless you made the trip as part of the support crew, nothing gives you a sense of the proportions of the journey – both ambitious and fragile – like the powerful documentary directed by James Moll. After watching the stunning film, you will either be motivated to mount some impossible voyage of your own, or be utterly intimidated by the prospect of even a short run on a sandy beach. Or both.

The movie isn't widely available – you probably won't be able to find it at Blockbuster – but you can pick up a copy on the Internet. There are also occasional screenings at which Zahab speaks about his experience.

Either way, if you're looking for inspiration, or just something to do on an inclement summer night, *Running the Sahara* is not just a documentary for and about runners, but a compelling film that rivals the drama of any Hollywood blockbuster. Hey, if a rainy day is getting you down, this is set in the desert, with not a drop of rain.

The production values are extraordinary. Perhaps that's not surprising since the director is an Academy Award winner. But given the conditions, the making of the film was almost as ambitious as the runners' journey.

When you consider how much went into shooting the expedition, it makes you realize the incredible bet the film-makers made that the runners would accomplish their impossible task. After all, there wouldn't be much market for a movie called *Running Some of the Sahara*.

The movie offers a long look into the mindset of the adventurer, an exaggerated version of the ordinary runner who sets an ambitious goal like a 10k or a marathon. Zahab, Charlie Engle and Kevin Lin don't seem to have any rational reason for deciding to run across the Sahara other than, as climber George Mallory once said about Mount Everest, because it's there.

Beyond ambition, another essential element, it becomes clear, is a supportive family. All three spouses, including Zahab's wife, Kathy, step in and out of the story line, and you can see the requirement that an ambitious explorer has for an understanding partner willing to accept the subordination of ordinary life to an obsession.

Some of the most emotional and hilarious moments of the film are when the spouses visit the runners and then have to leave again.

It's a nature film – the footage of the varied terrain of the

Sahara is absolutely breathtaking – and a travelogue. It's also a story about a group of men travelling in close proximity. If you've ever been on a road trip over thousands of kilometres, imagine how frayed your nerves would get with the mounting exhaustion, not to mention the aches and blisters, of running sixty or seventy kilometres a day.

That's clearly demonstrated in Engle, a charismatic, funny and narcissistic American who, as the expedition wears on, begins to browbeat and emotionally blackmail the support crew and one of his fellow runners who considers quitting.

The climax of the film comes when Engle suffers a leg injury in the final few hundred kilometres, and can barely walk. He suggests that rather than be slowed down by him, Zahab and Kevin Lin rest while he walks ahead, then run to catch up with him. But not long after they fall asleep, he starts running, setting up what amounts to a race to the finish line. Zahab's extraordinary drive, focus and positive attitude are revealed when he tells a frustrated Lin to conserve his energy for running. "We'll talk about it later," he says, as they start to push to catch up to Engle.

Were it not for *Running the Sahara*, the scope of what Zahab and his fellow travellers accomplished would be far less easy to understand. But it's more than just a story about an audacious expedition through unforgiving terrain. Because while the Sahara might be impossible for almost all of us, the relentless pursuit of a challenge, the turning of the impossible into the possible, is something every runner can understand.

[**36,680 STORIES**]

iRun to give girls a second chance at a childhood LARRY DEARLOVE, ONTARIO

At the finish line of a major running event, there are thousands of stories.

In May 2009, I decided not to run in my hometown event, the Ottawa Race Weekend. I'd participated each of the previous six years. But this time was different. My wife was eight months, three weeks and six days pregnant, just a nudge away from giving birth to our son. I didn't want to face a tough decision if I got paged in the middle of the marathon: should I try to finish first or cut it short and go straight to the hospital?

More importantly, I didn't want to face my wife if I showed up an hour after my son was born wearing a finisher's medal.

Instead, with a fully charged cell phone on my hip for hour after hour on Saturday night and Sunday morning, I watched the final steps of thousands of runners in the 5k, 10k, half-marathon and marathon. I saw little of the rest of their races: the nervous energy at the start line, the exuberant first few steps, the pauses at water stations, the walk breaks, the struggles and recoveries, the walls broken through, the boosts from friends and family along the course.

I saw nothing of their months of training: squeezing in the long runs, overcoming the injuries, fighting off the colds and aching pains and harnessing whatever motivation brought them to the start line.

Instead, I caught only a fraction of their journey. But it's not like reading only the last five pages of a book. You don't need to know the entire back story of a runner to feel his pain and joy in the final few metres.

Like Jason Warick, the Saskatoon marathoner who limped across the line with devastating leg cramps, then waved and blew kisses to a cheering crowd to say thank you for carrying him to the finish.

And the winner of the women's marathon, Asmae Leghzaoui, who crossed in a course-record time and then promptly threw up a steady stream of something the colour and consistency of a banana smoothie while organizers draped her country's flag on her shoulders.

And thirty-nine-year-old David Cheruiyot, who outfoxed the other lead runners in the men's marathon, then paraded back and forth over the finish line with the Kenyan flag on his shoulders, while a small group of his countrymen celebrated yet another marathon title for the homeland of distance running.

It's where you see Rick Ball suddenly sprinting past to finish in a world record 10k time for a single-leg amputee, just a few weeks after setting the marathon record in Boston.

And Mark Sullivan, the remarkable runner from Pennsylvania who has run 134 sub-three-hour marathons, and calls Ottawa his favourite, coming across in 2:47.

And a woman running the 10k, for whatever reason, in a fairy costume. And a pre-teen 10k finisher goofing off in the final few strides, leading medical staff to mistakenly think he was injured.

It's where dreams are achieved and broken. Like the group

of runners charging to finish the marathon in under 3:20, a Boston-qualifying time I know very well. And, at the other end of the spectrum, Liz Maguire, the Ottawa masters runner who was hoping for a personal-best in the marathon, but unfortunately reached the finish line a lot earlier than she expected, having pulled out after seventeen kilometres because of the flu.

And it's where journeys are measured not in finishing times but in dollars and cents, like for Steve Madely, a radio host who walked ten kilometres with his family in his quest to raise $400,000 for the Ottawa Regional Cancer Centre, where his wife is a patient.

And Gavin Lumsden, who completed his final marathon of twenty-six, one for each letter of the alphabet, in a quest to raise money for Ascent for Kids, a program to help underprivileged kids become active and avoid obesity.

It's where the impossible happens and you are almost moved to tears. Like when an hour and a half after the start of the 5k race, when 7,234 runners have already crossed the finish line, Jodi Graham, just three years after a near-fatal car accident, finishes the race with a group of supporters in pink shirts surrounding her and the crowd noise rises and spectators continue to applaud for what seems like five minutes as she walks the last twenty-five metres.

Standing at the finish line, it's hard not to feel the desire to run. But I made the right choice. Not long after we went to bed on Sunday night, my wife went into labour. I had fresh legs for the marathon ahead, and the next day our son was born.

$$\begin{bmatrix} \textbf{A FEW FOX FACTS} \end{bmatrix}$$

iRun to show my cancer who's boss DAVID MURRAY, ONTARIO

18: Age of Terry Fox when he was diagnosed with bone cancer in 1977.

15: Number of centimetres above the right knee that his leg was amputated.

3:09 Terry Fox's finishing time in the seventeen-mile Prince George to Boston Marathon race in 1979, in which he finished last but was cheered by most of the other participants who waited for him at the finish line.

101: Consecutive days in 1979 that Terry Fox trained before taking Christmas Day off as a present to his mother.

5,083: Number of kilometres Terry Fox ran in training for the Marathon of Hope.

5,373: Number of kilometres he ran during the Marathon of Hope.

17.7: Number of kilometres Terry ran on the first day of the Marathon of Hope.

73: Number of days Terry ran at the start of the Marathon of Hope before taking a day off.

143: Number of days the Marathon of Hope lasted.

5: Number of days Terry went without a shower while running in Quebec because neither he nor his supporters could speak French.

8: Number of shoes Terry used on his left foot during the Marathon of Hope.

1: Number of shoes Terry used on his prosthetic right foot.

10,000: Number of people who welcomed Terry to Nathan Phillips Square in Toronto.

$100,000: Amount of money Terry raised in one day in Toronto.

$12.70: Amount Terry spent on "sunburn lotion" on July 4, 1980.

$1: Fundraising goal, per Canadian, of the Marathon of Hope.

32: Number of kilometres Terry ran on August 30, 1980.

18: Number of kilometres Terry ran on August 31, 1980.

21: Number of kilometres Terry ran on the morning of September 1, 1980.

9: Approximate number of kilometres Terry ran on the afternoon of September 1, before asking to be taken to the hospital, ending the Marathon of Hope.

$10,500,000: Amount raised in a telethon on CTV just six days after the end of the Marathon of Hope.

24,100,000: Population of Canada in 1981.

$24,170,000: Amount raised by the Marathon of Hope as of February 1, 1981, at which point Terry's goal of one dollar for every Canadian had been achieved.

3,339: Number of times Jody Wright of Ancaster, Ontario wrote "I love you, Terry. Smile!" in a letter, one for each mile of the Marathon of Hope.

22: Age at which Terry Fox became a Companion of the Order of Canada, the youngest ever.

22: Age of Terry Fox when he died on June 28, 1981.

2,639: 2,639: Height, in metres, of Mount Terry Fox in the Rocky Mountains.

83: Length, in kilometres, of the Terry Fox Courage Highway, a portion of the Trans-Canada Highway between Thunder Bay and Nipigon, Ontario.

100,000: Estimated number of participants in Canada in the Terry Fox Run in 2007.

900: Approximate number of Canadian sites for the Terry Fox Run.

49: Number of other countries that have held Terry Fox Runs.

1,900,000: Number of people reported to have participated in the Terry Fox Run in Cuba in 2004.

$400,000,000: Amount raised to date by the Terry Fox Run.

3,000,000: Number of students, from more than 9,000 schools, who participated in the first Terry Fox National School Run Day in September 2005.

1: Amount Terry Fox said you could give in order to be part of the Marathon of Hope.

0: Entry fee for the Terry Fox Run every September.

$$\begin{bmatrix} \textbf{HOPE AND ANGER} \end{bmatrix}$$

iRun to feel powerful JOSEE PHARAND, ONTARIO

When I told people I had run the New York City Marathon in 2010, most of them had only one question:

"Did you see the Chilean miner?"

I didn't get anywhere near him. But I was touched by him all the same.

Edison Pena was the twelfth of thirty-three miners rescued after sixty-nine days underground. He emerged just weeks before the marathon and when race organizers found out he had been running every day underground, they invited him to watch the race in New York. He told them he wanted to run it.

He finished in five hours and forty minutes, walking most of the last half on bad knees. But he was celebrated in New York like a visiting rock star, a bigger hero than either of the winners.

It's not the fact that he completed the New York City Marathon. That was pretty impressive, given the shape he must have been in and the fact that his runs beneath the surface topped out at about 8k. Still, a marathon was a snap, a brief ordeal compared to what he had been through.

What struck me is the fact that he ran every day in that mine. When faced with fear, desperation, the prospect of death, Pena cut his boots down to the ankles to create make-shift running shoes. He ran until his feet bled. He ran in sweltering heat, in dark, claustrophobic tunnels.

The miners have sworn a pact to take a Las Vegas approach to the first few days after the collapse – what happened in the mine stays in the mine, one of them said on reaching the surface. But there is evidence that were desperate moments in the early hours. Some reports say the fear caused disagreements, even fistfights. One psychologist who observed their behaviour compared the scene to Lord of the Flies.

But when others chose to give up, he chose to run.

And what is running, whether on the ground or 700 metres below it, if it's not an act of hope? Hope that you can chase down a dream like a 5k or a marathon. Hope that you can change, that you can become something you never were before. Hope that you can get into better shape, one step at a time. Hope that there's a future ahead of you that's worth staying in shape for.

Faced with the news that they were trapped in a tunnel, with no prospect of being rescued for weeks, if ever, how many people would think, "I'm going to start running"?

Edison Pena did. He got blisters and sores until finally, after two failed attempts to smuggle running shoes down the shaft to him, the psychologists on the surface who controlled every bit of correspondence with the miners finally agreed to let him have a pair of Nikes.

For Pena, running was a demonstration of hope. Hope that he would make it out. Hope that there was something on the other side of this ordeal that was worth training for.

It was also an act of anger, as he wrote in a letter to a reporter on the surface.

"Why do I run? Perhaps it is because I have this fury. I could just lie down, but my fury has been channelled into a hatred towards this mountain.

"I wanted the mountain to get bored, seeing me run," he wrote. "I am not defeated. I am fighting. I feel that by running I am fighting to live."

When he arrived in New York, Pena said through an interpreter, "I was running to show that I wasn't just waiting around. I was running to be an active participant in my own salvation. I was running because I was also contributing to the struggle for our rescue. And I wanted God to see that I really wanted to live."

Aren't we all running, in our own way, to show that we're not just waiting around? We run both to improve and to prove.

It might not be as pronounced or as urgent as Edison Pena's, but we all run out of a mixture of hope and anger. Hope that we can progress, that we can sustain our health. Anger that our bodies sometimes hold us back from the dreams in our hearts, that we are fighting aging in a battle that we will inevitably lose.

We all have our mountains.

[**YOU'RE GOING TO BOSTON**]

iRun in hopes of getting to Boston DON DYER, ALBERTA

Running is an individual sport, but I like to think this is a story about teamwork.

Depending on how you look at it, I am either too slow or too young to run the Boston Marathon. While dozens of athletes reached the Holy Grail for amateur runners in April 2009, I was at home. But even so, I had a Boston story of my own.

I have been blessed with the good fortune of having a friend who runs at exactly the same pace as I do. He happens to be ten years older than me, so running at our speed, my friend is a lot closer to hitting his Boston-qualifying time than I am.

A few years ago, when we ran together once in a while, my friend tried to qualify for Boston and came up a few minutes short. I ran another marathon around the same time and was reminded once again that until I aged a decade or so, Boston was out of reach.

So, what would be my next goal? If I couldn't get to Boston myself, I decided I should strive for the next best thing. On a routine run not long after our marathons, I threw out an idea: my friend and I would train for a marathon together with the goal of finishing in his Boston-qualifying time. If all went well, he'd get in and I'd have an excuse to do another marathon, some company along the way and maybe even a personal-best, though still-not-good-enough-for-Boston time.

We started our quest in late 2006. Our goal seemed realistic, but something always got in the way. In 2007, my friend broke his collarbone while cycling, putting him on the disabled list for a couple of months and cancelling our next planned race.

The next winter and spring, our training went very well. We did almost every run together and stayed on course through tempo runs, speedwork and long runs. Along the way, we talked our way through the plans for what would become his next bestselling book and my latest business venture.

We ran together so often it became, well, a running joke. Each of our wives started saying, "It's your boyfriend" when the phone rang. We were just slightly ahead of the times. The bro-mance comedy *I Love You, Man* was still a year away (for the record, we did not go see it together).

All signs were pointing to a successful marathon. But three weeks before race day, on the eve of our last long training run, my friend learned from his doctor that he had an infection in his heart. It wasn't quite as serious as that sounds, but there was to be no running for at least a few months. Once again our race and his dream were cancelled.

Our plan had been to do the Mississauga Marathon. Throughout our training, I had always pictured running it together, so when he pulled out, I almost did the same. But he convinced me to go ahead and I finished in my fastest time ever, a few minutes under our goal time. It didn't get either of us into Boston, but it proved our training could produce the result he needed.

That fall, we ramped up our training again. And this time, finally, we made it to the starting line together. On race day in Cumberland, just outside of Ottawa, we made a deal. If he hit a wall, I would stay with him and try to pull him along to the finish. But if I started struggling, he would go ahead without me. We ran together for thirty-two kilometres, then I started getting painful leg cramps. Over the next few kilometres, I watched him get further and further ahead, disappointed to be falling behind, but satisfied to see that he was still on pace.

I struggled on and, with a few kilometres to go, learned he had made it with a few minutes to spare. I had only one goal for the race and we had made it. My only disappointment was that I didn't cross the finish line with him. But after I finished a few minutes later, we celebrated with our families for the rest of the day.

When I used to run by myself, I often pictured striding to the finish line of a race, feeling strong and crossing in a fast time. But once we started training together, with a new goal in mind, my vision of that final stretch changed. I pictured a celebration in the few final hundred metres, during which I would point out loudly to my friend that he was finally, after several false starts and years of training, on the verge of making his goal.

In time, I think I'll get my own shot at running the most coveted race of all. But even if that never comes, it was still a milestone for me that my running buddy achieved his goal when he finally went to Boston, reaching the end of a long journey we began together almost three years earlier.

So let me say now what I planned to shout if only we had crossed the finish line together in his qualifying race:

"Bob, you're going to run the Boston Marathon."

[FINISH LINES]

iRun because quitting is not an option JENNIFER ROSS, ONTARIO

There is just something about finish lines.

I like the nervous energy at the start of a race. I like the first few hundred metres of an early-morning training run when I breathe in the fresh air and feel the sense of possibility. I like turning for home at the midway point. I like pushing myself, testing my limits through the second half of a tempo workout or a long run.

As you can probably tell, there is not much about running that I don't like. But there is nothing better than the finish line.

Does it have anything to do with that joke about running? Some people say running is like hitting your head against the wall: it feels good when you stop. In other words, the best part of a run is the point when you don't have to anymore.

On some days, maybe. There are long training runs during which the only satisfying part is when the struggle ends at your doorstep. There are races in which the appeal of the finish line is that it means the pain finally will be over.

But those are the exceptions. Most of the time, when I'm approaching the finish line, that's when I start to feel like I could run forever.

In almost every race I've entered, no matter how exhausted I might have felt even five minutes earlier, once I see the finish

294 WHY I RUN

line, my mood is transformed into excitement and expectation. The roar of the crowd, that final destination in sight, the sense of accomplishment – they all lift me to a new energy level.

Even on a training run, when I hit that final, familiar stretch through my neighbourhood, my frame of mind always changes. I'm almost home. I've got this.

Sometimes when I'm running alone, my mind drifts to those final few hundred metres of a race. I can picture the archway across the course, the clock ticking away the seconds as I approach. I can feel my energy rising, my pace quickening. Even though I might be in the middle of a routine 8k run through my neighbourhood, I get chills just thinking about it.

Maybe it's because with the end in sight, you can afford to turn up the pace a notch or two, to stop holding back and saving something for later.

Maybe it's because that's when the celebration begins.

The finish line is an accomplishment. It's a triumph. It's the realization of a dream, the fulfilment of a promise. It's another task checked off, another unit of work done. Even if it's just a nice and easy 5k, you left the house with a target in mind and now you've achieved it.

Unlike most things in this world, a run has a beginning and an end. So much of life is complex, unfinished and grey. Running is black and white, binary, simple. It has a start and a finish, both clearly marked. Performance matters, but for most of us, the biggest thing is just whether we got it done or not.

Despite all of that, it isn't stopping or completing that I relish. I never actually picture reaching the finish line, only approaching it. I've run that final stretch toward the finish a million times in my mind, but I've crossed over it only in the physical world.

It's not the actual finish that inspires and energizes me, but the promise of it.

There is joy in approaching the end of any journey, when you're not quite there but you know it's within your grasp. Printing out the final few pages of the university thesis. The day before your wedding. The morning you start your dream job, or those final few weeks before retirement. It's the intersection of anticipation and realization, of hope and fulfilment.

When it's over, it's over. But when the finish line is calling from a few hundred metres away, its voice is loud and powerful and alluring. I'm not finished, but I'm almost there. And I've got it. Nothing can stop me now.

$$\left[\text{ MY LAST RUN } \right]$$

iRun because one day I might not be able to BRENDA CUGGY, ONTARIO

I don't know when it will be. I don't know why it will be. But someday, there will be a last run.

When I started jogging around the neighbourhood, even when I trained for my first marathon, I wasn't certain how long I would keep running. Maybe after a time, or having crossed a finish line and checked it off my list, I would switch to another activity.

But once the repetition engrains it into your lifestyle, rewires it into your DNA, it becomes hard to imagine not running. Today I dread even the idea of an injury sidelining me for a few months. I picture myself going stir crazy watching other people still running blissfully by while I wait out a recovery.

So the prospect of giving it up permanently is something I push to the farthest corner of my mind, the place for those topics that are especially hard to confront, like: "Which of the Two of Us Will Die First?" or "Colonoscopies."

But it must be so. Everything has a beginning and an end, and there will come a day when I will never run again.

I stop short of saying that one day I will no longer be a runner, because I like to think that even when I'm not running, I'm still a runner. No matter when you retire, can you ever stop being a coalminer or a soldier? Once something becomes part of your life,

298   WHY I RUN

it remains etched in your character even if you let it lapse from your routine.

I wonder sometimes what specifically will make me stop. Though it's hard to picture now, it's possible I may just give it up. Maybe due to a variety of factors my running will dwindle over a few years and one day I just won't be doing it anymore. That must happen to a lot of runners. The motivation slips a little, you grow a little older. Maybe you take up another sport. But before you know it, you haven't been for a run in weeks. Then it's months, then years.

It could be that I get injured and never recover well enough to run again. I could get warned off running by a doctor. I could get sick.

And there is another possibility to consider: Will it be my last run because my life, not my running, gets interrupted? Like everyone else, runners die for more reasons than just old age or prolonged illness. Sometimes it happens suddenly. No matter what it does to improve our cardiovascular system and delay this and forestall that, running offers no guarantees.

I'm optimistic I'll be running in my fifties. But what about my sixties? The numbers, at least in terms of race participation, seem to drop off significantly there. Will I be one of those rare people still running when I'm seventy? Shuffling along at eighty? Even if I'm blessed with extraordinary luck and health, at some point it must end.

And before it does, there will be one last run.

Unless I feel a tweak or a twinge that day that leads to something serious, or I plan my retirement like some professional athlete on a farewell tour, it's more likely than not that I won't know it's my last run until much later. In all probability it will be a routine run, nothing out of the ordinary.

It goes without saying that I want that run to be as far in the future as possible. But more important than the timing, I want it to be a certain kind of run.

About once or twice a month, usually in the final kilometre as I head for home, for just a few moments I think about what I'm doing. I think about the air I'm breathing, the movement of my legs and the feeling of good health I get from a respectable run.

It often happens at a time when I've had to deal with something frustrating or unexpected. For maybe the only time that day, I'm living in the moment, enjoying what it feels like to throw one foot in front of the other, just as a child might.

I pick up the pace a little and feel a little bit of pride that despite a busy life I've managed to stay in decent shape, good enough that I can head out the door on any given day and run for an hour or more without stopping.

And that gives me peace. And hope. And energy.

I pray that it isn't soon. But no matter when it is, I want the last run to be this kind of run.

As the final turn approaches, I think to myself, not everything in running and life is as I wish it to be. But it could be a lot worse.

After all, I'm alive and I'm running.

[**ACKNOWLEDGEMENTS**]

I'm quite astonished at the role running has assumed in my life and to discover that I have so much to say about the subject.

Ten years ago, I never would have predicted that I would one day think of myself as a runner, much less write a book on the subject. But since my first group run in a marathon clinic, I've been inspired by other runners to go farther and faster and to write about my experiences and theirs.

So I'm grateful, first and foremost, to the many runners with whom I've shared this journey. Some of them appear by name in this book, many others have impacted these pages in less obvious but equally meaningful ways.

I'm thankful, too, to the citizens of iRun Nation, who inspire me with their passion, engagement and their own words, which appear throughout this book.

Much of the writing in *Why I Run* is adapted from columns that have appeared in the *Ottawa Citizen* over the past five years. I want to thank the *Citizen* and editor-in-chief Gerry Nott for allowing me to draw on that material for this project and for giving me the opportunity to write about running in the first place.

I want to thank Ray Zahab and Tania Jones, two athletes I admire deeply and whose accomplishments I could never match, for the privilege of running with them and sharing a love of the sport. Their advice, support and guidance have been invaluable on both this book and iRun.

I'm very grateful to Malcolm Gladwell. Getting to run with one of my favourite writers, at least for a short time before I fell behind, was special. Having him write the introduction to this book is a tremendous honour.

Lisa Georges has been my creative partner on this book and iRun since the magazine was launched. She is an incredibly talented artist with great vision, and also a good friend.

I'm also appreciative of the small group of people who have read through drafts and made suggestions for this book, including Bruce Deachman, Karen Karnis and Jessica Aldred (who convinced me there was nothing wrong with making it more about me, a concept I initially resisted).

My running partner and cherished friend Bob Plamondon, a best-selling author himself, not only appears regularly in this book, he has also helped shape it as a sounding board, editor and strategic adviser over so many runs while this project has taken shape. Thank you, Bob, for sharing not only this journey but many others.

Nothing I do would be possible without the support, encouragement and inspiration of my family. I am thankful for the legacy of my big sister, Dianne, who loved unconditionally, was generous with her time and took pleasure in the simplest of things. What more to life is there than that?

I am indebted to my parents, John, who taught me a love of language, writing and editing, and Florence, who still teaches me a love of life.

I am deeply grateful every day for the blessing of the children in my life: Erica, Jack and Bump. iRun to keep up with them and to stay healthy enough to see them flourish for many years to come.

I started this book with an anecdote about my wife Ginny's observation on the role of running in my life. Far more non-negotiable than running is my love and gratitude to her as my best friend and partner. She is the biggest reason both why and how I run, and without whom any journey I take would neither be possible nor worthwhile.

Mark Sutcliffe

April 2011